An Iridescent Life

Essays on Motherhood and Stepmotherhood

Marcelle Soviero

Acknowledgements

Some of the essays in this book originally appeared in the following publications: Anderbo, Babble.com, Eating Well, Literary Mama, More.com, New York Metro Parents newspapers, Salon.com, StepMom Magazine, The Story, distributed by American Public Media and National Public Radio, Tiny Lights, Upper East Side magazine and Wilton magazine.

*For my husband Eric and my children
Luke, Sophia, Olivia, Jamie and Johnny.*

Contents

Garden Party

My oldest daughter, Sophia, turned five one month after her father moved out. I planned her fifth birthday party with the obsession only a newly separated mother could bring to such a task, pouring everything into the details that would make my girl happy, as if a party could make up for the events of the last month.

We'd told Sophia and her younger sister and brother about the separation over a breakfast of chocolate chip muffins. We explained that Mommy and Daddy would not live together any more. "Not ever," my husband said, following the therapist's instructions to make it final, leaving no room for hope. I spent that first month shuttling Sophia and her siblings back and forth to visit her father at a hotel.

Then, for three nights in a row, I stayed up late at the kitchen table, making 28 pink daisy invitations to be mailed in paper flower pot envelopes, my first try at origami. I cried as I folded those envelopes, remembering Sophia's fourth birthday, a huge gathering with both sides of our family—two doting grandmothers, her father playing "Happy Birthday" on the violin.

My party plan involved dozens of Gerbera daisies the children would plant in large pots they'd paint themselves. I would set up different activity stations in the backyard: pin the petal on the posy, pipe cleaner flowers. Every hour at my desk at work I came up with another idea; a catch-the-butterfly game, daisy chains, pinwheels. Lunch would be tulip-shaped cucumber sandwiches with edible blossoms served from terra cotta pots, along with raspberry-lemonade tea in flower-patterned cups I'd purchased from Goodwill.

The Saturday of the party I woke at 4 a.m. The rain was torrential, flat sheets of water dropping from a sky as grey as a cookie sheet. I went outside on the deck in my slippers, my cup of coffee quickly filling with water, my eyes filling with tears. I came back into the house soggy, exhausted. I could not catch my breath as I swept out the garage, our new party site. I hung the flower piñata from the rafters, shoveled potting soil into large buckets, and lined up dozens of colorful daisies on fold-out tables.

Cursing as I hung yellow birdhouses from the kitchen ceiling, I blamed myself for the weather and everything that had happened to our family. But as I looked at those buckets of potting soil, I couldn't help thinking of Sophia as one of the flowers. She had grown inside me, and despite the storm that had destroyed much of our old life, it was up to me to set her roots good and deep. The more I thought, the more I decorated. I filled the kitchen with tissue paper bouquets and wrapped flower-power notepad favors to tuck inside watering cans in the wheelbarrow now set up in the living room. I blew up God knows how many balloons, until I grew dizzy, then queasy.

I was sitting on a chair, head between my knees, trying to breathe, when Sophia came into the kitchen, wearing her pink party dress and click-clack shoes.

"Happy Birthday Party Day," I said and hugged her. "It will

be an indoor party, even more fun!" Smiling, she ate her flower-shaped pancake. When I took Sophia into the garage, she gasped, her brown eyes wide, and looked from floor to ceiling. "The flowers are winking," she shrieked, pointing to the bright yellow daisies.

I gathered her to my lap, her small shoulder blades peeking out from the back of the polka dot sundress, I wove her long hair—she had been born with so much of it—through my hands. I looked at the garage walls. "The walls are too drab," I said. "Let's paint them." Sophia hopped off my lap and I pulled out the bin of acrylic paints meant for the party. I handed her a stash of paintbrushes. "Make whatever you want, my beautiful girl," I said, pointing to the long grey wall. Sophia painted a series of flowers with smiley face centers. Above her flowers I painted a rainbow.

Sophia is in the ninth grade now. We were looking through her school scrapbooks recently when she paused at the photo of herself blowing out candles at that long-ago garden party.

"You made a butterfly-shaped cake," Sophia said. "Remember, we painted the garage?"

"Do you remember anything else?" I said.

"There were so many kids and you whacked the piñata open because it wouldn't break. All of those girls, and we still couldn't smash it."

"Anything else?" I wondered if she remembered that it was the first party we had after her father moved out.

"What do you remember?" she asked.

I remembered the rain cracking against the garage walls, and the loneliness, for myself and my children. But now, I also remembered the birdhouses dangling, the flowers winking, and how, when the piñata finally broke, candy fell and the small silk flowers inside fluttered to the floor around my girl, like lucky stars.

The Wee Free Children

"I want to kiss the girl who fought the Fairy Queen with a frying pan!" I say, hands stretched toward my giggling five- and six-year-old daughters. Sophia waves her magic wand then fashions fairy furniture with the lid of a shampoo bottle, three toothpicks, and a paperclip. Olivia, busy with her reflection, tries to un-pucker her flannel pajamas where we'd rubber-banded the fairy wings.

"Mirror, mirror on the wall," she begins, adjusting her tiara, confusing her fairies and princesses.

My son Johnny—"baby Jingle," as his sisters call him, though he's almost two now—bobbles into the bedroom in big boy underwear. Sophia tapes a pillowcase to his bare back, making a cape.

"Jump! Jump for joy! That's how you fly, silly," she says, taking hold of Olivia and Johnny's hands. They jump and shriek, as if Johnny Jingle just might take off.

The rumpus is my own fault. The children are, no doubt, in sugar shock from the microwave mudpies—chocolate slices glued with marshmallow fluff, garnished with graham crackers.

We're at least on our way toward sleep, I tell myself, not wanting to tamper with the spell that seems to unravel in the room now, each minute strung together like pearls.

Seamlessly, the girls waltz Johnny to his room across the hall, declaring night-night for him. I follow, tossing a Tonka truck and toy soldiers from my path.

"Happy hugs," Sophia says, hopping onto Johnny's bed and giving him a squeeze, his small blue room lit with a lightsaber lamp.

"What's your grateful?" Sophia says and Johnny puckers his lips. "I'm thankful for Petie," he says, squishing his stuffed lizard tightly under his armpit.

I am grateful that this is my weekend with my children, every minute of it precious. I mark my weekends on the calendar like forget-me-nots—with me, with-me-not, with me, with-me-not. Since my divorce six months earlier, the children spend every other weekend with their father, falling twice a month into a rabbit hole.

After Johnny's goodnights, we walk back to Sophia and Olivia's bedroom. I tuck the girls into one twin bed, two heart-shaped faces peeking out from beneath the princess sheets. Though there are two beds in the room, my Irish twins sleep together. I round off the evening with a chapter of A Hat Full of Sky, perfecting my imitation of Ms. Weatherwax and Nac Mac Feegle.

It's after 10:00 when I step into my red, cocooned bedroom with its timbered ceiling and slanted pine floor, hallmarks of this old home, the only kind I'd consider buying in spite of everyone telling me to take a townhouse. Decisions had to come quick once the divorce was final, and perhaps I hadn't thought it through, purchasing a house based on its having a fairy window, a carousel horse mural, and a climbing tree at the edge of our yard.

Window open wide, September air balloons into my bedroom. I am tired in the way only a single mother of three young children could be, the ache in my bones, the knots in my spine like stuck keys on a piano.

I climb out of the window onto the flat roof. The full moon is centered between the branches of the climbing tree. The stars spill like sugar. I breathe the air in and take a sip of wine from a sippy cup. I think about the less-than-perfect morning, following Sophia through the house, pretending to clean while she tapped a light switch ten times and centered and re-centered a throw rug on the wood floor, carefully pressing it back into a perfect oval. She is an anxious child since the divorce—and I am a guilty mom.

It had been my decision to cut the family into two unequal halves. I see in my mind the yellow laminated bus tag pinned to Olivia's backpack, the large letters and numbers: BUS NUMBER 23, so she knows which bus to take to which house. I see the word "divorced" on Johnny's preschool application.

Then a voice: "Mommy?" Two faces peer out at me from the window. "What are you doing, Mommy?" Olivia says, as Sophia boosts her up so she can climb out onto the roof first. "I'm taking a time-out, Livvy-Boo."

"Can we have a time-out?" Olivia asks, walking tightrope style, though the roof is not at all steep, Sophia close behind. My lap is instantly divided, one little girl on each side. A soft wind nestles into the creases between our bodies, the smell of lilac swells the air.

"Which one of you can't sleep?" I say. I know one woke the other.

"She can't," they say in unison, pointing fingers at each other.

What would someone say if they saw us on the roof—almost midnight? And what did it matter? Our lives were no longer stacked neatly into drawers but maybe it didn't need to be that way. People divorced; my children would be okay. Sophia was already queen of the cakewalk, Olivia already the fairest princess of them all.

I did not rush to get the girls back into bed. Instead I slid the moment into my pocket like a shiny penny, recognizing this might not happen twice, the three of us on the roof like this, waiting, as it were, for the cow to jump over the moon.

Divorce Photo

Outside the courthouse, signed divorce papers in hand after a yearlong custody battle and proceedings that left me in financial ruins, Larry, my new ex-husband asked a stranger to take our photo. I was shocked, and though I hated him for what he had put me through, for some reason I stayed still as he put his arm around my shoulder like a football buddy. It was raining; I wore a blue cashmere sweater. A woman with maroon lipstick snapped a shot of us on the courthouse steps.

That we could stand together even for a moment was miraculous, given the lawyers and lies. Given Exhibit A of the Property Settlement Agreement, an Excel spreadsheet detailing what was his and what was mine. And Exhibit B, the visitation schedule for our three children, aged one, four and five at the time.

That was nine years ago. I think of that photo as I pluck items from the memory trunk I keep in my office. I wonder how we might have looked, in those moments after the divorce, when our life was a drizzle, and the rain fell like so much broken glass.

I wonder if Larry still has the snapshot—and why he ever asked someone to take a picture in the first place. Maybe that was closure for him, a seam on the day once the camera clicked.

The man I married and had three children with is minimized to a shoebox inside my memory trunk now. There's a photo of us with the ship captain on our cruise to Portofino. A photo from our December wedding—all those poinsettias. And the card Larry gave me for our first anniversary. "Love you forever" he wrote on the pop up heart; I bend it back into the box.

Why do I keep this? I wonder. Perhaps I want my children to have access to items that prove their father and I loved each other. I imagine Sophia, our oldest daughter, finding this note I wrote to Larry after I became pregnant with her. Maybe these sealed mementos will supplement the images she must have of her father and I dropping her off at one house or another, or standing like stick figures at her Back to School nights.

What's left from my first marriage, in addition to the children, is what's in this box. That's why I can't throw any of it away. It's proof to me too that I was married to my first husband for eight years, and there was some good in it.

Yesterday, I ran into Larry at our local Starbucks. I was in front of him in line. "Buy you a soy latté?" I said, surprising myself with the offer, and surprised that I still knew his drink. Though we communicate weekly about the kids on email, I hadn't actually seen him for months; I studied him. His dark hair had thinned and he'd grown sideburns flecked with grey. I tripped on my oversized umbrella.

"Lot of rain lately," he said.

"A lot," I agreed.

We sat for five minutes, even though the kids weren't there and we didn't have to pretend. "Sophia's a teenager now," I said, awkwardly.

"She is," he said.

"Olivia starts lacrosse next week," I said. I went on like this, though I wanted to ask how he was, really. I was remarried, but he was not. Did he have someone?

Looking at him, I thought how hard it had been all these years, living five miles from each other but rarely speaking, trying to raise three happy children from two very different vantage points. When we were married, in my mind, he was not an involved father but I thought now how he had become one, different from the one I expected, but a father for sure. I probably should have told him that. But instead I asked where he got his umbrella. "I like the color," I said, though it was plain grey.

Wrapping my hands around the paper cup, I wondered what someone looking through the window might see, if it was somehow obvious that we were a couple who was married once, had three children together. Oddly, I wondered what would happen if I asked someone to take our photo now, how it might compare to the divorce photo on the courthouse steps. Would we scoot our chairs together and smile—and feel it this time, eight divorced years behind us? Would the lines in our face be harder from the years, or less so since we live apart?

I come back to our flat conversation, stay inside safe words, afraid to trigger any of our hot issues. "Well, I have to go to Stop 'n Shop," I say. Larry makes an excuse to leave as well. We walk to our separate cars, the rain falling, the puce sky the color of bruises, mending.

Meeting Luke

Eric pulled the Jeep into the driveway. Luke – the brown-eyed boy I had heard so much about—popped out of the car, raced to the backyard play set, and slid down the slide. He was so exuberant that I raced after him, gave him a high-five and took a turn on the slide. Luke had Eric's thick head of hair; brown curls that touched his eyebrows, and Eric's wide and easy smile, minus the two front teeth.

Eric and I had decided it was time for our kids to meet. We'd been dating for five months and between us, we had five kids age seven and under. My three, Sophia, Olivia and Johnny, and Eric's son and daughter, Luke and Jamie. Luke, age seven, was the oldest of the bunch. I was the most nervous to meet him, thinking he was the one old enough for me to leave an impression.

That Saturday morning I had woken at 5:00 a.m. and made a labor-intensive lasagna for lunch. I changed my outfit three times, and changed Sophia, Olivia and Johnny's clothes twice as well, until they all whined. Johnny, just two, wriggled in his new khaki shorts and button down short-sleeve shirt. Eric had driven from his home in Connecticut to my home in New Jersey and had arrived at 10:00 a.m., right on time.

Luke continued to race around the yard and down the slide and I took a turn with him. I gave him a hug—a little squeeze really—at the base of the slide. This gesture could have been a disaster. Luke might have pulled away and left me embarrassed in front of the other children who were still standing by the car in the driveway, watching us.

But Luke gave me a little squeeze back then shouted, "I'm fast!"

"Race you!" I said and we doubled up and did a lap around the swing set. My son Johnny toddled toward us shouting "Fun! Mommy! Fun!" Luke tried to lift Johnny onto the swing, while I coaxed Eric's daughter, Jamie, and my two daughters out to play. The girls hadn't spoken yet. Instead, they stared at their shoes.

But within an hour, the five kids had turned the playset into a theme park, splashing down the hose-drenched slide, shrieking "Water World!" as they looped in circles through the sprinkler. "Careful—not too fast!" I said to Luke who I was sure would slip in the puddle that had formed at the base of the bucket swing. That is how I began my mothering of Luke.

Later over our lasagna lunch, Luke told us about the long-tailed skink and fire-bellied toad he kept back at his dad's house. The other kids were already looking up to Luke—a role Luke would play for years to come. "I want toads, too, Mommy!" Johnny said. As the sun spread on the pine table where we ate I daydreamed what it might be like to have two more children, a son and daughter, who age-wise fit right in between my own children.

That June, Eric and I threw a party for Luke's seventh birthday and I met Luke's mother, a beautiful bow-mouthed woman wearing a slim black skirt and heels. I had spent the day pitching tents for what would be a campout sleepover party and never changed from my mud-streaked jeans and t-shirt. Embarrassed about the way I looked, I shook Erica's hand and told her how wonderful her children were.

I made a frog-shaped cake for the birthday boy. "I never had a frog cake!" Luke said. Next I brought out mud cups—crumbled brownies with gummy worms, and that pushed Luke into sheer delight; I caught his happiness and made it my own. The kids played with water guns and when one boy got too aggressive, I instinctively blasted him with my plastic pistol, protecting Luke.

Eric and I married each other two years later. Luke, the little boy who had since that first day come crashing into my life, was our best man at age nine in his seersucker suit jacket and slacks. Before he walked with Eric down the grassy aisle in our backyard where the ceremony was held, I gave him a hug and I thought about how we'd hugged that first day I met him, and how he had become, in two short years, a boy I would do anything for.

Luke is 15 now, a six-foot-one high school sophomore; we've made it through book reports, bad grades, detention and dirt bikes. But because I don't have the final say in most decisions— he has a mother and father—I bond with Luke in ways I can't with my biological children. Luke and I have room to relax, space enough to be friends. We've watched countless reruns of Law & Order and have had popcorn-filled nights watching the Die Hard and Terminator movies, just the two of us.

Luke, a football player now, is still as full of energy as when I met him. On the way to practice the other night, Luke and I listened to my favorite song by the Crash Test Dummies, track number seven, "I Think I'll Disappear Now," a song I referred to—only with Luke—as my former marriage theme song. "It was horrible with my ex," I said, something I would never say to my biological son who was enamored with his father. "If you can, find the love of your life the first time," I said. We talked about Lisa, his friend who is a girl, our best conversations always happening in the car where eye contact doesn't exist.

That same night, after practice, Luke, and a group of his friends, shaved their heads to raise money for kids with cancer. I had signed the paperwork for the school-sanctioned event the night before. "You look like a pencil," my son Johnny said when we picked up Luke. I thought Luke looked like a good-looking gangster.

"You look awesome," I said, but I could tell Luke already missed his locks. "It'll grow back honey," I said, giving him a hug, this boy, my friend—now almost a man.

Blended

The bus carrying our wedding party and most of our guests was an hour late getting to our house, the spot we'd chosen for the ceremony and reception. Eric and I waited. Today, after three years of dating, we were getting married, joining our hearts, homes – and five children—Johnny, Jamie, Olivia, Sophia and Luke, ages four to nine. Our little quintet would be our wedding party. And they, too, were stuck on the bus.

The children had been excited since our engagement five months before, wondering where we'd go on our honeymoon. After the announcement, we all moved into the historic Henry Finch house circa 1842, Eric and I having passed on purchasing one of the cookie cutter colonials that had closets and updated plumbing. The Finch House had character: thick moldings, a Harry Potter closet under the stairs, and four chimneys to give Santa options. All this and our own slice of the Saugatuck River, which cut through our backyard, where there was now an arbor, rows of wooden white chairs, and a piano set up for the ceremony, which was supposed to start an hour ago.

With the children at the hotel the previous night, I'd imagined a leisurely morning, a long hot shower, a chance to comb my hair. Instead, I was a sack of mud until noon. Eric and I moved the trampoline, in the drizzle, to the neighbor's yard, and while Eric fixed the party tent that had blown down in last night's storm, I drove Lemon, our oversized Brittany Spaniel to Dog Gone Smart, the pet hotel, since he gets hyper around a host of people. Lemon was short a shot (required for admission), so I'd raced him to the vet and waited an hour for Dr. Noonan to immunize him.

Eventually I did get dressed. I wore a fitted ivory gown, nipped at the waist. The gown held every inch of me in except for my calves, where the dress flared, producing, what I felt now, was the look of a mermaid, not the look of an hourglass, as my mother had convinced me in the bridal shop. I'd curled my long blonde hair, normally straight as uncooked spaghetti. I put on pink lipstick. Then, feeling I had to jazz it up somehow, I tried the false eyelashes, ultimately flushing them down the toilet in frustration. Other than those lashes, I did not fuss much. I had no time. Until now. As I waited for the bus.

I stood at the kitchen window in the mermaid gown. The servers flew in and out the screen door, keeping the salmon crepes warm, moving everything into a second kitchen they'd set up in the garage. I took a small sip of scotch. Straight from the bottle.

Clearly, at some point in the wee hours I'd fallen through the rabbit hole and, like Alice, woke in a nonsensical place with strange characters that surrounded me now. The Justice of the Peace, a top-heavy middle-aged woman who I had a bad feeling about from the start—but who was available on this date, paced in the living room, tapping her silver wristwatch. The DJ, a substitute for the man I hired, blew by me. "Everything's cool!" he said, positioning his ponytail.

I was a spectator in my own home and I did not fight it. My

sister-in-law, a woman who can manage twelve tasks at once, breezed by holding organza bows and a hammer. "You look beautiful, Marcelle," she said. Antonio, the cook, passed by "Bellisimo Marcello!" he said, blowing me a kiss and waving the carving knife he'd finally found. I laughed out loud, feeling sillier by the minute in the gown. I took another small swig and considered changing into my jeans.

Out back, the river swelled with rain and the September air swooned with the smell of butterfly bushes, penne pasta sauce, and a hint of hornet spray. Dozens of our local guests sipped blue martinis in the backyard, under the fixed white tent whose tiered tips poked into the late afternoon sky.

At last, a wheeze.

The Lakeside bus pulled up along the fence, taking up half the street, stopping cars in both directions. The people in paused cars watched my beautiful children, wrinkled, but finely dressed, race in the front door.

"Mommy! Your hair is excited!" Johnny, just four, said, his hand in the pocket of his pinstripe seersucker jacket, his light-blue tie touching his belt buckle. He was referring, I think, to the curls in my hair. "I ate twelve Twizzlers and two gobstoppers on the bus," he said passing me a purple jawbreaker he'd held the entire ride, which now made a lavender stain on his palm. I popped it into my mouth.

The girls swooned around me like bees to a petal. "Mommy, you're a fairy queen," Olivia said, touching a thin line of beads at the waist of my dress. "My eyes dropped to Sophia and Olivia, ages nine and eight and my step-daughter Jamie, just seven, in mismatched white dresses they'd chosen from the sale rack at the Lollipop Guild. Just last night, they'd tried the dresses on again. Dancing debutantes, spinning in front of the full-length mirror in my bedroom, skirts blooming. "It's hard to believe I'll love you even more tomorrow than I do right this minute," I'd said to them.

The guests filed into the folding chairs and Leonard Bernstein's "Make our Garden Grow" played through the speakers, the notes gently pulling Eric and his little best man, Luke, beside him.

They walked down the makeshift grassy isle, in matching blue blazers, a slice of sun catching the silver in Eric's hair. I remembered our first date at the SoHo Grande, two hearts winking tears, lips in a kiss under a plaid umbrella. He was the good guy in every movie I'd ever seen, the one the Hollywood starlets wished they'd chosen once the bad boys broke their heart. He was mine now. Always would be.

Jamie entered stage left, her click-clack shoes tinkling the slate pathway, tiara tucked into a blonde bun. Awestruck by the crowd that now filled the chairs, she forgot to drop even one of the silk flower petals from the white woven basket, though for weeks she'd practiced throwing big bunches at a time. Johnny, the tiny ring bearer, followed close behind steadying the ring on the small pillow I'd stitched from the plaid flannel robe my father wore for at least 30 of his short 56 years.

My maids of honor, Sophia and Olivia came next, holding hands, their long dark hair, secured with faux diamond clips, scrolled down their backs. The children surrounded Eric at the arbor. I took them all in, considered my life in that instant, not precisely what I had planned, but perfectly imperfect.

My brother, who'd be my stand-in father today, walked me down the isle, and placed me before Eric like a teacup. Eric and I said our vows to each other, then to the children. Eric's family, veterans of the theater, performed our wedding song and my nieces read Jack Prelutsky poems. My father–in–law, Ed, a man who saved Shakespeare in a small Vermont village, read Sonnet 116, something he'd done at every Feidner Family wedding for decades.

We are married almost six years now. We celebrate our anniversary family style. "The day we all got married," Johnny, a ripe young man of ten, likes to say.

The Boy Who Is Mine

I load four of my five children on the school bus; now it's just Johnny and me. We've entered "Johnny Time," the half hour each school day morning that I have to spend alone with my youngest son, a small-for-his-age first-grader. Since the divorce, Johnny spends one morning a week at his father's house, so I appreciate this special time with him even more.

"Ready Mommy?" he says. "Ready!" I say, and, unless we're rained out, we head outside to play baseball before his bus comes. It is late autumn, the leaves have let go of the trees, and I stand in the grass in my pajamas and robe, a cup of cold coffee on the ground next to me. Johnny races to get our mitts from the garage, his little muscled body pulsing with excitement.

I throw him a high fly; the ball crashes through the branches of our oak tree; he zig-zags beneath the limbs judging exactly where it will fall. "Johnny Jingle makes the catch," I scream and he beams, raising his mitt, calming the crowd. "How did you get to be such a great baseball player?" I ask, TV-interview style, using a small stick for a microphone. He says the answer I made up for him. "I owe it all to my mother!"

He bats next, my pitch lacks accuracy but he slams it. He hits left-handed—the way my father, a professional baseball player and also named Johnny, used to. Johnny does nothing else left-handed, but by some odd coincidence he hits lefty and his swing makes me smile every time. He has an uncanny resemblance to his namesake as well, tufts of blonde hair, blue eyes like light blue fondant.

I throw a thousand balls, or so it seems by the time the bus lumbers to our front gate, letting out its routine wheeze. Johnny gives me my three kisses, left, right, and center, before getting on. And though I am tired, feeling thin as wax paper, I know I did the right thing seven years ago.

Because Johnny was all my idea. The baby I insisted on having, though he was conceived at a time in my life when a baby should have been the last thing on my mind. My marriage was breaking, my daughters were just two and three, and my career had hit high gear. But for reasons I have only begun to figure out, though I know it was more than a desire for a boy who I could name after my father, I wanted a third child as much as I'd wanted the first; every cell of me committed to it, the need innate, primal.

My husband Larry and I were in marriage counseling at the time; we had been for two years. The therapist cautioned against having another child just then. "Another child will not fix things," she said. Of course not, I thought. But that was not the point.

The point was I wanted a third child whether my husband and I stayed together or not. I was clear on the issue in my mind. I told my mother I was pregnant first. Unlike the blissful announcement of a baby the first two times, my mother's smile taking up her entire face; this time, she met the news with a blank expression. "Why?" she said, before hesitating, then hugging me as if to hold me up.

I knew what she was thinking; she was the one who came to stay with me when I suffered postpartum depression with both of my daughters, who were born in the context of a better marriage than what I had now. She was the one who took Sophia from my lap while I cried, leaving me frozen in the polka-dot rocking chair, cold cabbage leaves on my breasts to sooth the engorgement. And she was the one who knew I was unhappy in my marriage now.

I waited many weeks before I told other people, including my husband, who shrugged then smiled, when I showed him the stick flared pink that proved my point. After I told Larry he left to go to his flying lesson. He would fly 15,000 feet in the air while I stayed grounded.

Larry was home less often. He'd had so many interests and made time to pursue them all—a zest I loved when I married him but hated now that we had children. We were together less and less, a thick silence webbed between us. The girls sensed the end of something; clinging to me, grabbing at my thighs while I cooked macaroni and cheese again, my stomach huge, wedging into the countertop as I filled the large pot with water. At any time I could snap, like a celery stalk, knowing that if I didn't unravel during the pregnancy, chances were high I would plummet again right after the baby was born.

It was a lonely pregnancy, punctuated by doctor appointments that I went to by myself. At 21 weeks as I lay in the dark on the exam table, my melon-sized belly in full bloom, I asked Dr. Davis if it was a boy or a girl. "I thought you didn't want to know?" he said, having delivered both of my daughters who I insisted be a surprise. I felt the baby roll inside of me, swimming, as it surfaced on the ultrasound.

"I want to know," I said.

"Boy," he said.

"For certain?" I said. It was certain.

The divorce came when Johnny was 18 months old; I now have to share my son, along with his two sisters. On Wednesdays and every other weekend the children go to my ex-husband's house and the little bird beats in my throat, the catch of anger I feel toward a man, I believed, did not spend time with his children when he had the chance. I struggle to see the situation through a less resentful lens, thinking that perhaps the forced separations help me appreciate the extra minutes I have on weekday mornings with my son, before the bus comes—the little boy who I still like to believe was all my doing.

The Living Museum

I peeled the paper off the back of the faux mustache and stuck it above my daughter's upper lip. Olivia would be Milton Hershey for the third-grade Living Museum.

"Chocolate has changed my life," she'd said when she made the choice. It had been a downright tie between Milton Hershey or Tom Carvel. I'd suggested a few famous women, ones we might easily find books about for the actual report. Madame Curie, Helen Keller. No dice. "But you're a girl" her older brother, Luke, who'd been Babe Ruth just three short years ago, said. Olivia dug her sneakers in, she would be Milton.

The chocolate-related choice was not a total surprise. Born with a sweet tooth, Olivia wished for chocolate, not coins, from the tooth fairy. She kept details about her chocolate factory in a purple three-ring binder in her bedroom. The binder held her secret formula for a pink chocolate bar, the inner foil yellow, not silver. "Pink for me, yellow for you," she said when showing me the formula, that I pinky swore not to reveal. "You can eat the wrapper, too," she said. On subsequent pages she'd made detailed drawings of her chocolate bakery, a castle-shaped shop edged with M&Ms and Twizzlers. "I love the peanut-butter-cup door handle," I said.

Over the weeks, Olivia researched her subject. Indeed, we learned Milton Hershey invented the Hershey bar in 1901, and the Hershey Company makes 100 million Hershey kisses per day now. The thumb-sized silver-foiled domes are called kisses because the machine that makes them "kisses" the conveyer belt. We learned that Milton failed with caramels but brought milk chocolate to the masses, while also being a great philanthropist, establishing a renowned school for disadvantaged boys still in existence. At every juncture Milton chose a different direction from the pack, breaking the mold so to speak. Not unlike my daughter, I thought.

Eventually Olivia finished the report and corresponding project—a poster, with real candy bars hot glued to the border. She worked hard. Tonight would be the dress rehearsal for family only. We finalized her outfit: Luke's grey pinstripe suit jacket and slacks. She stepped into the too-big dress shoes and I swabbed the lime-green nail polish off her nails. "Milton didn't wear nail polish, Boo Bean," I said, the nickname having come from her sister Sophia, just 18 months older, who met Olivia in the hospital at birth, pressed her nose and said: "Boo."

I bobby-pinned Olivia's long brown ponytail to her head, and stuck the sprouting ends under the black derby hat. I thickened her eyebrows with eyeliner, something she'd done at an earlier trial run with a black Sharpie marker. The clip-on tie completed the outfit. "Lets hear it, Milton," I said.

It was quiet and we sat at the table, Olivia's two brothers and two sisters having been bribed with ice cream—with chocolate kisses—if they'd just sit and listen. "You hold the index card Mom," she said. "Make sure I get it right. Word for word." Then she asked me to push her button, a red circle sticker on her right hand. "This is my play button," she said, pointing to the red dot. "You push it and I talk." I pressed her button.

"Hello. I am Milton Hershey. I had many successes and failures in my life, but I kept trying." She spoke her five lines without a miss. She then bowed twice, a little too emphatically, and the mustache flew off, landing on her shoe like a black caterpillar.

In the morning, the parent paparazzi snapped pictures as several dozen eight-year-olds filed in to the south gym, forming a rectangle around the basketball court. The sun splatted on the gym floor. I spied Rosa Parks and Neil Armstrong in a pow wow with Pocahontas. I sipped my Starbucks. I forgot about the conference call I had in 42 minutes.

Mr. Arbunkle, team leader for the entire third grade, gave clear instructions, noting the red-dot sticker on each child's hand, the play button. "Start with your child. Press their button to start their monologue. Listen, then move clockwise to the next child," he said. Apparently this would not be a parade across the stage with each child speaking one at a time, but a simultaneous broadcast. "It will get loud with all the children performing at once," Mr. Arbunkle said. Then there was a great pause, a hush in the room as he cleared his throat and looked heavenward at the ceiling rafters. "Thank you for letting me work with your kids," he said. They are the future leaders of America."

True. I looked among the children, transformed into some of our nation's greatest historical figures, each with their own eight-year-old history. Among these bright faces were children who would discover cures for diseases, invent new ways of time travel, and foster world peace. And Olivia, future owner of a chocolate empire, might one day employ thousands, donate chocolate to the masses. She might build a town, an amusement park and a school for disadvantaged children, like Milton himself.

My eyes welled as I walked toward Olivia, who stood now with

Emily Dickenson to her left and Amelia Earhart to her right. I pressed her play button. She spoke her lines slowly and clearly. She'd practiced speaking up and not speaking too fast and she did it. I beamed. I hugged her, thankful she was still young enough to like hugs even in public. At the end of her speech she took a Hershey kiss out of her suit jacket pocket and gave it to me. Olivia had been dead set on a handout and I had to get previous permission from Mr. Arbunkle, I was so glad I did, the way she took that chocolate out like a little treasure for each listener.

I made the rounds. I stayed too long. I'd stopped to listen to almost every child. I'd do my conference call from the car, I thought, slowly stepping back to my daughter one last time before the bell rang. I stood before her, my little queen of the cakewalk, my little Boo Bean. I reached for her hand, not to press the play button this time, but to hold it. To look into her brown eyes and freeze this moment, that would be, I knew, part of our personal history.

Grow-a-Frog

I hid in the marble bathroom stall at Cipriani's conference hall, surviving among other things a sketchy cell phone connection with the Gilly Hotline at Grow-a-Frog headquarters. I'd just checked in for a seminar attended mostly by men and I knew I'd have privacy in the ladies room. "My daughter's tadpole has not come," I shouted into the phone. "Can you please track the tadpole?"

The woman on the other end asked for my zip code. I repeated it. A pause. "There's a cold snap in your area. We can't ship our froglets when it's that cold," she said in a syrupy southern drawl. I negotiated, which is what I do for a living. "Can you make an exception? Can you send two in case one dies?" I started to give my credit card number. "I can't mail a Gilly Tadpole in this weather," the woman said, stunned. How dare I assume that the fine folks at Grow-a-Frog headquarters could forgive even one dead tadpole?

I pressed on; my primal instinct to please my children in

extreme ways had become worse since the divorce. I could not control the weather, I thought, but I could control the arrival day. "When you send it, can you make sure it doesn't arrive on a Wednesday?" Silence on the other end. If the tadpole arrived on a Wednesday Olivia wouldn't be home to open it, she'd be at her father's house. Tadpoles need to be opened immediately upon receipt. I'd have to drive the box over to her father's house so she could open it there and he might take the credit.

The Grow-a-Frog was all my idea. The world's best gift for Olivia, my frog-loving daughter. Her passion inspires greatness among her four siblings. Once, upon seeing fuzzy frog slippers at Wal-mart her younger sister insisted, "I'm getting those for Olivia, I'll use my allowance." And, I admit, wherever my work takes me, with each airport I race through, I seize the moment to purchase the frog keychain or froggy shot glass.

Olivia is my middle child. Naturally sweet with an impish sense of humor we all cluster around. Nine months out of the year, rain or shine, she's by the river that runs through our backyard. Pippi Longstocking in mud boots up to her knees; frog net in hand, notepad in her back pocket. When she finds a frog she instinctively blots him with a paper towel; like a bitty baby out of the bathtub. Then she inspects, classifies, and names him, cataloguing the new friend in her notebook. Once done, she'll run to show the frog to anyone who happens to be nearby. While we've become a bit numb to the ritual, she delights in the catch every single time.

She is the kid who asks for nothing, but this birthday when I asked her what she might want, she actually answered: "I would like a frog please Mommy" she had said, yanking up her size 7 slim jeans that hung on her, despite the sparkle pink belt. She continued with the specifics. "An African Bullfrog, which is also called a Pixie Frog." This was news to me. There was such a thing as a pixie frog?

I Googled frogs and was immediately thankful she had not chosen, say, the Gastric Brooding Frog or Mexican Leaf Frog, both termed as exotic and in the case of the former, possibly extinct. Shortly after sorting through more than two dozen varieties, I was smacked with the fact that frogs of any kind feast on live crickets. Further, if it was a small frog we'd need to feed it live bloodworms placed in a milk cap. This would require nightly runs to Fido's Food Bin to purchase handfuls of insects and possibly worms in Ziplock baggies. I imagined darting home from work, bag in hand, watching Olivia feed the frog live feed. Is this the kind of mother-daughter moment I was hoping for?

Eventually I came upon the Grow-a-Frog website. My interest peaked. A Grow-a-Frog tadpole morphs into a frog before the naked eye, its clear skin allowing an intricate view of the entire cycle. Olivia would be able to see its pinprick heartbeat by peering through the frog's temporary ecosystem, a six-inch acrylic box. The best part: Grow-a-Frogs eat dead food that looks like sand. Then, no food at all while the legs grow in. Midway in the growth cycle, the froglet eats just one nifty nugget, a quarter of the size of a chocolate chip, twice a day. There were add-ons down the road: Frog buddies and oyster beds, and truly odd: magic powder that when sprinkled into the habitat inspired the frog to "clap." This was doable I thought. I placed my order.

On March 12th, Olivia's birthday, she opened the frog kit; a precursor to the actual frog. I explained she was going to grow her own frog. She clutched her chest. No other gift mattered. She filled out the official frog adoption postcard that guaranteed a tadpole would arrive within five days, pending the weather. She darted out to the mailbox and carefully positioned the postcard. The next day when she arrived home from school she asked: "Did my frog come Mommy?" her chestnut hair spilling past her shoulders, her big brown eyes dreamy at the mere possibility. Fifteen consecutive days passed. No frog. I called twice a week.

During those fifteen days, Olivia kept a running roster of possible names. At dinner she collected votes, a new name each night. Some considerations: Tinkerbell. Hamlet. Fritz. She kept her overall list secret, so we never knew the front runner. In the end, the stars aligned and Olivia's tadpole arrived-- as luck would have it-- on a Friday. She flew in from the bus and saw the box marked "Live Specimen" on the kitchen table. "It came?" she squeaked. "My froglet came!" She was winded, I guided her into a chair. She uncorked the 6-inch Styrofoam tube and peered in telescope style. "It's still alive. It survived shipping!" she squeaked, her brown eyes a bit watery.

Olivia's four siblings, my husband, and Murphy McDonald, who happened to be over for a play date, gathered around Olivia at the kitchen table. She eased the clear plastic bag out of the cylinder, holding her breath, an ever-so-adorable-scientist-in-the-making. She let the bag hang from her fist and we all cocked our heads to get a glimpse. The specimen, small as an inchworm, thick as a thumb, was translucent with greenish innards. It's miniscule lungs, mere pencil dots on its gill cavity. "It needs to acclimate" Olivia said, her finger on the "Arrival Day" section of the instruction pamphlet she'd read and highlighted. "Here you go mister frog," she said, positioning the bagged tadpole up next to the acrylic box that she'd filled with spring water and festooned with fairy-sized sprigs of plastic seaweed.

"What's his name?" I asked. Olivia sat back down in her chair again, elbows leaning on the table, her chin cupped in her hands. She was thinking. I sensed she'd been inspired in a new direction, given the tadpole's striking physical features. "Snot" she said. "His name is Snot."

Popular

"Citadel," I say.

"A fortress," my daughter Sophia says, then uses it in a sentence. "My room is a citadel." She moved into her own bedroom a month ago, when she turned 12, and it became clear she could no longer share a room with her two younger sisters.

Sophia's room, once antique white, is now a blinding lime green, lit now by just one lamp. It is almost 11:00 p.m. Sophia is the only one still awake. Her hair smells like coconut shampoo. The still wet strands, recently cut into layers, stick to her cheeks.

Sophia tucks the two textbooks into her backpack, then takes a second backpack from her closet. She stuffs her socks, soccer uniform and an outfit for Monday morning into the second bag. She squeezes the bulging pack between her thighs to get the zipper zipped. Tomorrow Sophia will sleep in a different bedroom, at her father's house. I consider my childhood spent in one home, tucked in by a father and a mother together.

Sophia is used to the every-other-weekend packing, but I'm

not. The second backpack bothers me, a fat reminder that Sophia does not have the fairytale childhood I'd planned for her, that her father and I have been divorced for half of her life already.

"I'm not popular, Mom," Sophia says, as if randomly plucking the words out of the air. Sophia's back is to me, her oversized T-shirt comes well past her knees. She has always been small and tonight she seems even smaller, looking barely 10.

I pick the Abercrombie jeans up off the floor and toss them toward the wicker hamper. "What's popular?" I say, trying to make time to find words that will fix everything all at once for Sophia, always my first instinct.

"Popular?" she repeats, with a look that says: Mom, you know this. "Popular girls sit at one lunch table. They're the pretty ones. They've all been asked out or are going out with one of the popular boys," Sophia says. "They don't even talk to me; it's like I'm invisible."

Putting Sophia to bed used to be much easier. The words "popular," "citadel," "Abercrombie," not yet part of her vocabulary. We used to read The Paper Bag Princess, her favorite story where the princess, dressed in a paper bag, rebuffs Prince Charming. Like the Paper Bag Princess, Sophia, a diminutive dragon slayer herself, never cared what others said. Never gave one whit about what the prince thought.

I'm angry at these middle-school princesses. I put my arm around my oldest daughter who has always been a source of comfort for me. The daughter who, at age five, seeing me in despair after her father moved out, took my hand, brought me out to the swings, and showed me and her baby sister Olivia how to kick clouds. I see Sophia in my mind now, hopping off the swing, walking back towards the house, her shoulder blades like clothespins under her sundress.

"I don't think I'm invited to Rachel's party," Sophia says. I am quiet. I consider how I solved this when Sophia was in second grade. The year we moved to a new town after the divorce, and I dropped her in a class that already had its cliques: so-and-so played with so-and-so at recess. Sophia was left out. But I'd fixed it, inviting all the girls to our house to play, serving drippy ice cream in pastel bowls. Sophia shined, leading an excavation of old stones in our backyard, encouraging the girls to dig knee deep where the old barn had been. Sophia had scooped the ice cream into the five bowls herself, and put glitter toothpicks on top, one for each friend.

I could say now, "Sophia, you're the prettiest," the way my mother used to say to me, the words that never worked because as a child I could only think of course my mother would say that. Or, I consider my father's approach, his emphasis on perspective, when a party invite did not come or a friendship dissolved. "You won't even remember that girl's name a year from now."

"Remember your stuffed duck, Daisy?" is what I say, thinking that a story where Sophia is the star may be what's needed. "You were 3," I say. "You took an egg from the fridge, snuck it to your bedroom, and placed it under your pillow.

"I put Daisy the duck on top of the pillow," Sophia says, and I'm relieved she's joining in and not rolling her eyes at me.

"And that night, when I tucked you into bed, gold yolk oozed onto the sheets."

"I thought the egg would hatch," Sophia says, and laughs. "I tried it again the next night."

"You always had your own ideas, Sophia," I said, sad that somewhere between when she was six and now, Sophia stopped believing stuffed ducks could lay eggs.

I tuck her into bed, sheets to chin. "I wish to grow an inch," she says, a joke of ours since she wrote that in her letter to Santa in first grade. I push her hair back, and trace the freckles that stretch from one cheek to the other, a narrow trail over her small nose. When I was little I didn't like my freckles, but of course I love Sophia's.

I sit on the edge of the bed and turn off the lamp. I know Sophia is moving into a new phase where I can't solve everything with a Popsicle or play date. In this new place, Sophia has to believe in herself and I have to believe that in spite of the second backpack, the second house, my second marriage, Sophia will find her own way. Tomorrow, she'll get on the bus, weighed down with two backpacks and a violin. She'll sit at the popular lunch table. Or she will not. She'll be invited to Rachel's party. Or she will not.

"When I have a party, Mom, I'm inviting everyone," Sophia says, turning towards sleep.

Something Is Always Missing

"We have six minutes," I say, my head under my son's bed, looking for his red baseball shirt. It's 7:50 on Saturday morning, and Johnny, age eight, sits mournful on his bed. "I already checked the closets," he says, shirtless, his lips pressed together in one line.

Today's the big game where Johnny will pitch for the first time, his debut on the mound, and I can't find the red shirt. "Wilton Phillies, 11" it reads. "Number eleven is the best. Number 1, then number 1 again," I said when the coach handed out uniforms and Johnny didn't get his favorite number, 3.

I forage and feel tears push up through me. I know the shirt is at Johnny's father's house. It never made it into the backpack after the game last Saturday, when Larry had him for the weekend, and I never double-checked.

My son, my sensitive son, will be the only one on the field today wearing the wrong shirt, looking different from the other kids, disadvantaged from the start because I don't live with his father.

My children have gone to more games and activities unprepared than I can count because I can't keep track of what is at which house. There is no way to plan for what I don't know I won't have at any given moment. But still I try, stuffing soccer socks and football jerseys in backpacks, not wanting my children to be short-changed, singled out.

I'm angry, no doubt about it. The logistics of divorce are exhausting, and often I feel like I'm stuck handling more than my share of them. I'm always the one to drive Johnny to and from my ex-husband's house. Though I am only sometimes the forgetter, I am always the fixer, or at least try to be.

Last Saturday afternoon I drove to Larry's house to drop off Johnny's clarinet and pick up his football cleats. Larry did not answer the bell, and he had not left the cleats out. I propped the clarinet case against the doorframe. These trips take everything out of me. Even after so many years, it doesn't feel normal to leave my children's things on a back porch. Later that day I watched my son play football in the rain, the only one in sneakers, not cleats, a poorly prepared Wilton Warrior, and I couldn't help feeling responsible.

Back in Johnny's bedroom, I open and close the left-hand dresser drawer where the shirt should be, expecting a different outcome every time. "I'm sorry, Champ," I say, slamming the drawer harder than I mean to.

My daughter, Sophia, excavates clothes from the hampers, checks under pillows. "Call Dad," I say. "Ask him to bring the shirt." But I know Larry won't answer his phone at this early hour, and he likely won't come to the game.

"Look for any shirt that's red," I say. Sophia looks. She is a teenager now and rarely follows my instructions, but she must sense my anxiety. As must Johnny, who sits on his bed quietly, pulling at the laces on his mitt. This is my one child who is still enamored with me, a special mix of a boy, exceptionally athletic and especially sensitive, and I am letting him down.

We are five minutes late for the baseball game. Johnny runs to the dugout wearing a red Gap T-shirt. "We can't find his uniform," I say to the coach, holding my breath and Johnny's hand. "Can he still pitch?" He can.

Larry arrives in the bottom of the seventh inning; he carries a Stop 'n' Shop bag containing Johnny's shirt, still dirty from last week's game. I race to the dugout from my spot behind first base and hand Johnny the shirt. "It's okay, Mom," he says. "It's too late."

Johnny strikes three out in the last inning. My little boy is resilient, a winner. Still, I wonder how he feels out there on the mound, not a number 3 or an 11, but the only numberless boy among the numbered.

Mom. Stepmom.

The curtain opened and my ten-year-old stepdaughter Jamie, stood center stage; a serious Missie Mouse with bouncy black ears and polka dot vest; her face etched with white whiskers.

I'm wedged now in a seat between the two "real parents" Eric on one side and Jamie's mother, Erica, on the other. Jamie, Rosie as both her mother and I call her, speaks her lines then sings the wee mouse song. As she sings, I think of our morning drives to camp; Jamie rehearsing her songs, her voice an adorable alternative to the radio.

At intermission, Jamie comes out to greet us, spinning toward her mom first, then her dad. I am last for the hug; I feel duck-duck goosed. I whisper into Jamie's mouse ear, "You're the best one up there, honey."

And as I look at her pale face, my friend Susan's voice comes to mind: "Of all five kids, Jamie is the one who looks most like you." I think she is right.

Jamie turns back toward her mother, who reapplies Jamie's lipstick, and I am reminded of so many times when Jamie has left me behind. Times when Jamie and I go to Luke's football games and I sense Jamie waiting for her mother to come. Her bounce off the bleacher when Erica appears. It bothers me every time, though I know Jamie should like her mother best. They have a good relationship and part of my job as a stepmother is to champion that relationship. But Jamie and Luke live with me much of the time and it's not easy.

Motherhood and even more so, stepmotherhood, is the hardest job I have and my roles as mother and stepmother are the organizing principles in my life. I was redefined when my son and two daughters were born, but shortly after each birth I settled into the word: Mother. But even after all these years of being a stepmother, I have not settled into a definition—except to say that I am not the mother.

And since I am not, since I am always the third person present at teacher conferences, violin recitals, award ceremonies and sporting events, when someone compliments me on Luke or Jamie, I can't take the credit; worse, I feel labeled as the stepmother—at risk, at any time, in anyone's eyes, to be seen as the stereotypical evil "step."

And I do have evil thoughts. Just a week ago, home with the five children, Eric away on business, Jamie came home from school with lice. As I separated her from the other children, parboiled the hairbrushes, and combed the nits out of her long blonde hair, I thought, "She isn't even mine and I'm doing all this." I wanted to send her to her mother's house for the night. I hoped my anger would not come out in the way I pulled at her tangled hair, thick with the lice-killing foam. Later I checked in on her and found her finally asleep, snuggled into clean sheets, smelling like peroxide and mint from the stringent shampoo. I kissed her cheek. "Rub it in," she whispered, and I rubbed the space on her cheek that I had kissed, something I always did when I put her to bed at night.

I remember a day not long ago that I spent with Jamie at our Girls' Lunch, just the two of us, Sophia and Olivia with their father. Sitting at a table at the Tuscan Oven, teacups before us, I poked my hand into a wicker basket of corks on my left. Holding one up I said, "What can you make with a cork, Rosie girl?"

"A Christmas ornament," Jamie said. "A pirate ship," she went on, and I saw myself in her, her imagination working so hard. After lunch we went to get our nails done at Angel's Spa—blue polish for both of us—and I drove home feeling guilty that my daughters were with their father.

I try to spend alone time with all my children, but I admit that me divided by five leaves less of me for my three kids, and I wish at times that my attention could be solely for me and my son and daughters, not diluted with two more children. But then I think of the large family Eric and I have, how lucky we are that the kids live with us, and I am happy.

At times I even find myself defending the family we have created. At a dinner party last week a skinny woman asked, "How many children do you have?"

"Five," I said and she calculated the ages, each child about 18 months apart. She continued asking questions, until I said two are my stepchildren. "So really you have three," she said, sipping her martini.

"No, really five," I said.

Looking at this woman, I feel unacknowledged. But there have been so may rewards too. It seems like just last week when I went to Jamie's first-grade classroom for Author's Day. Standing before the class, Jamie, an actress even then, read her poem about the princess and the bee, and I felt sure she was taking after me and my love of poetry.

After the reading, Jamie took me on a tour of the classroom. She was bright with pride in her tie-dyed shirt, showing me her math facts, her dragon lore. Last we walked over to the "I Am

Special" wall. I spotted her self-portrait right way, her hair yellow and everything else purple and pink, her favorite colors, even now. Below the crayoned face, she had written the words, in her best print letters: "I am special because I have a stepmom."

Hall-of-Famers

"In here!" my son Johnny says, pulling me into the Babe Ruth room at the Baseball Hall of Fame, pointing at the Louisville Slugger Babe Ruth no doubt swung to hit one of his 714 career homeruns. We walk through the rows of display cases; Johnny's enthusiasm building as he examines each artifact.

Johnny's passion for baseball is an ongoing pleasure for me, a sign of how my father lives on through my son. Johnny is named after my father, who died young of heart failure five years before Johnny was born. Dad played AAA baseball for the Red Sox; a southpaw pitcher. As Johnny and I walk through the museum I imagine snapping a photo of him with his grandfather; my father's large arm over Johnny's shoulder, buddy style. Instead, I snap a picture of Johnny next to a life size painting of Hank Aaron.

I wonder what my father would think of my little boy, so much like him, who hits left-handed and who can strike out the side in any given game. Though my father rarely talked about his baseball career, I imagine maybe in this setting he would tell Johnny everything, all the stories I heard secondhand after Dad died.

I brought Johnny to the Hall of Fame for spring break, my four older kids home with my husband. Having Johnny to myself was a unique occasion for one-on-one time with my youngest son. I'd booked a hotel with a swimming pool. I wanted to make it all special, squeeze every memory I could from the trip. I'd even told Johnny, just for this weekend, I would be a Yankee fan like him, instead of my usual role as a Red Sox fan. "Babe Ruth played for both teams," Johnny had said, giving me some leeway, "but let's be for the same team, Mommy, okay?"

Johnny wore his baseball mitt the whole four-hour drive from Connecticut to Cooperstown, reading Sports Illustrated for Kids on my iPad, reciting some stats from the backseat. We drove down one-lane roads, through small towns—Cobleskill and Broome, past Hubcap Heaven and the Cob Knob Driving Range, ramshackle houses pinpointing the start of another town.

When we arrived in Cooperstown, we parked near the batting range then walked through low hanging fog down Main Street, past rickety shops that displayed baseball memorabilia in dusty windows. I gave Johnny quarters for bat-shaped gumballs. We reached the Hall of Fame and started our tour on the second floor watching a ten-minute movie in the Grand Stand Theater, which was made to look like Comiskey Park, complete with stadium seating. The show ended with images of baseball cards projected onto the ceiling. My son looked up, his mouth wide, and I imagined my father looking down at him. I felt a combined love for my son and my father at the same time.

My father loved baseball season, and it was baseball season now. Johnny's Little League had started and I volunteered to be the "lady coach" as the boys called me. I had stood on the field with twelve third-graders wondering why I took the job, but I knew like so many things, I did it for my father, because he had been a coach and taught me what I know about throwing a baseball and keeping both hands down for grounders. And maybe Dad could see me, and my son, together on the field.

After going through 200 years of baseball history in the museum we went down to the official Hall of Fame on the first floor where Johnny raced to find the bronze plaques for his favorite inductees. I took three photos of him in his Yankee Cap next to Babe Ruth's plaque. Afterward, we went to the gift shop and I bought baseball bat pens for our Little League team and spoiled my son with pennants, pencils and so many packs of baseball cards.

Back at the hotel, Johnny, the only eight-year-old I know who watches ESPN, turned on the TV and opened his baseball cards, praying for Babe Ruth. "Will Grampy be in one of these packs?" he asked, just to please me. The first pack was all duplicates of cards he already had, same with the second and third packs; mostly dupes. "I'll trade them," he said, trying to stay hopeful, and I knew I'd be the lucky recipient. I'd long taken to trading baseball cards with my son as a pastime.

Johnny saved the World Series pack until last, frantic for Babe Ruth. He stopped mid-flip. There was Babe, in his Yankee uniform. Johnny looked at the card, it seemed too much for him. He separated Babe from the pack, laid him on the table and took a photo of the card with my camera. I congratulated Johnny on his good luck. It seemed, even with all the museum attractions, this moment with the Babe Ruth card was the highlight of his trip.

"Time to go to the pool," I said.

"I can't leave," Johnny said. "Someone might take my baseball card."

"Lets keep it in the gift shop bag," I said, holding the bag open. But he secured the card in a sheath of plastic that had been wrapped around the hotel glasses, and brought his treasure to the pool. Shirtless, in his bathing suit and baseball cap, the two of us took the elevator down. I sang "Take Me Out to the Ball Game" and Johnny sang parts along with me, raising his fingers for the one, two, three strikes your out refrain.

That night Johnny slept with Babe Ruth under his pillow. I dreamt of my father. Unlike most of the dreams I had of Dad, where he is nettled with tubes as he had been in his final days, in this dream he was young and strong in his Red Sox uniform, just like the photo I keep of him on my desk.

In the dream, my father and I played three-way catch with Johnny in the backyard. "Our boy can throw Martie," my father said, calling me by the nickname he gave me, which I haven't heard since he died. The dream was so real it was hard for me to wake into the new day; my head foggy, I saw the outline of my son in his Yankee pajamas asleep on the bed next to me, and swore I saw my father there too.

The Seder

I rang the doorbell of my ex-husband Larry's house, a jar of gefilte fish in one hand, boxed coconut cake in the other. To date, I'd been to the house on Thunder Lake only to drop off the kids. But today I was here with my husband, Eric, and two stepchildren, Luke and Jamie, for Seder dinner.

Given the circumstances, this was miraculous: I'd last seen Larry three weeks ago at the trial. Six years after our divorce was final we'd gone back to court over the religious upbringing of our three young children, Sophia, Olivia and Johnny. I'm Catholic; Larry is Jewish.

Eric, Luke, Jamie and I stood on the front steps. I did not want to ring the bell again. "Cool house," Luke, 13, said, looking heavenward to where the white columns we stood between might end.

"We could leave," I said.

"Just breathe, honey," Eric said.

"Tell me again why I'm here?"

"For the children," he said, taking the jar of gefilte fish and squeezing my hand.

Eric had been here for me each odd step of the journey. He'd been at the first meeting with the rabbi more than a year ago, where I sobbed, explaining I was the primary caretaker of my baptized children, and I could not raise my children Jewish.

Sophia answered the door, welcoming me as a guest in her other home. The divorce agreement said nothing about religion, so Larry and I tried to figure out Sophia's faith in real time. Each decision we made would mark her, and be the precedent for her sister Olivia and brother Johnny. But looking at Sophia, I knew Larry and I had not damaged her permanently yet. She stood at ease in the foyer. She'd grown into a beautiful girl with her father's dark eyes and my mother's wide-lipped smile, her mane of black hair a gift from some former generation.

Now in a house where my children lived when they were not with me, images of their life with their father came into view, the backpacks on each hook, three jackets hung in the closet, a drawing with the words "I love my Daddy" in a frame on an end table.

I remembered a five-year-old Sophia in the tub with her little sister just after the divorce. The girls played in the bath bubbles, splashing suds onto their chins Santa-style, and spun the rubber ducks on the surface of the water, like dreidels, singing in Hebrew. That was how I first found out that Larry had been taking the children to Temple on his weekends. He had never taken the children to Temple in the eight years we were married.

I had fallen in love with Larry at a Seder at his house when we were dating. I'd grown up in a cloistered Irish-Italian family, a plaid-uniformed Catholic schoolgirl. I had never been to a Seder and at that one I met a Buddhist and a Muslim. As the conversation developed into a theological discussion, my mind stretched past Sister Marianne McCarthy into the realm of rabbinical texts, the Tripitaka, and the Quran. My world cracked open over a candlelit table with plates of beef brisket and roast turnips. My then husband-to-be was worldly, 15 years older than

I, and seemed to believe in all religions, subscribing to none.

We walked to the main room. "I come bearing gifts," I blurted, handing Larry the gefilte fish and coconut cake. Several children raced through the house and a few other couples greeted us. I knew one woman from the gym.

"It's so nice how you all get along," she said, nodding toward Larry, then Eric. "So nice how you're all here," she added, her words echoing beneath the cathedral ceiling.

All of us getting here was a long story. One that began with a two-sentence e-mail I received 18 months earlier stating Sophia was enrolled in Hebrew school and her bat mitzvah was set for June 12.

My ex-husband's e-mail, in its brevity, seemed a decision to change the course of my children's lives without discussion. It set off a series of sparks that turned into blue-flamed anger, then action; two motions filed within two weeks, followed by a trial.

In court I sat on the bench with my lawyer, waiting for our case to be called. I shuffled papers, my hands shaking, the children's baptismal certificates fluttering to the floor. Larry sat several rows in front of me, with a string of witnesses shoulder-to-shoulder.

Larry's lawyer called me to the stand. I swore to tell the truth and nothing but the truth. I considered another oath I'd made before Larry, to love you in sickness and in health all the days of our lives.

The lawyer fired off questions.

"Do you know how long the children have been attending Temple?" he asked. "Have you ever taken any legal action up until now?"

I hated him, catching me on a hook like that. No, I had not taken legal action, but I had built a case with Larry outside of the court. We'd tried to talk, but the words crisscrossed before ever being heard. The talking turned into pithy e-mail exchanges, what we each thought the other's intent was for the religion of the children when they were born. I believed we'd agreed the children would be raised Catholic and Jewish. My problem at this juncture really boiled down to a bat mitzvah. A ceremony that would confirm my daughter in the Jewish faith, somehow separating her from me.

"Are the children presently enrolled in any other religious instruction?" the lawyer continued, tension in his voice. I thought back to my enrolling Sophia in CCD when we first moved, and how I pulled her out three weeks later. The change in homes and schools was stress enough for both of us. And I thought the allure of taking three kids to Temple would wear off for Larry.

Larry's lawyer repeated the question. "Are the children enrolled in any other religious instruction?"

I began to explain the three-week enrollment.

"Answer yes or no," the judge said.

"No," I said.

"When was the last time you went to church?" the lawyer asked. "Christmas?"

Objection.

Sophia's Hebrew school teacher came to the stand next. I had never seen this woman before. She addressed me from the stand: "Did I know Sophia already knew her Torah portion?" she asked. I did not know. That was the problem. Somehow this all happened in secret, on the one day a week the children spent with their father. The lawyer finished the show with a former next-door neighbor, who confirmed that, yes, he and his wife had attended Seders in the marital home.

Court was adjourned until a date two weeks from that day. Two more weeks. It would be unbearable.

My lawyer walked me to my car. I locked myself in, tears dripping from my eyes onto the leather seat. My mind reeled back to my childhood, me in that white dress at my First Holy

Communion. I had memorized the Our Father and the Hail Mary. I'd taken the Body of Christ for the first time and had gotten stomach sick. Years later I would say my Hail Marys in succession after confession with Father Amato, where I begged forgiveness for my 16-year-old sins.

Though I'd grown up with God, that confession would be my last in a formal setting. Once I went off to college and was away from parents who did not know if I went to church or not, I opted to not attend. By the time I met Larry after college, my faith was packaged into silent prayers at night, the ongoing giving of thanks in a private setting. I married Larry within 12 months of meeting him the first time. We divorced eight years later, to the day.

Larry and I both lost so much in the divorce. But afterward, I found Eric, and I wondered now, for the first time, if Larry had found religion. Perhaps Larry was not just pushing his Judaism to control me, but he'd come to believe in it. While I reestablished my roots in an expanding family, with Eric and my children and stepchildren, Larry may have found the roots of his faith.

Darkness fell, and all the other parked cars had gone. I tapped out the number of years Larry had been taking the children to Temple and Hebrew school. I tapped seven times on the steering wheel. It had been seven years.

I put the key in the ignition, wondering for the first time if I should let Larry win this one. I told myself that whether or not the children were mitzvah'd, they would choose for themselves one day. Unlike in my house where Christianity had been a given, never questioned, my children would have to think things through as they grew older. Even with a bat mitzvah, Sophia would have to question the two faiths that were rolled up inside of her.

In the morning I called my lawyer. "Settle," I said.

Later that week, after my ex-husband heard of the settlement,

I received an e-mail invitation to Seder at his house. "Please bring Eric and Luke and Jamie," he wrote. I thought about the invitation for more than a week and decided it would be best for the children if Larry and I at last appeared to be on the same page.

I took in the scene before me now: Sophia pulling out the Scrabble game, Olivia trying to hide the afikomen while everyone watched. I went to the kitchen to pour a glass of wine and found myself alone with Larry in the kitchen. "It's a nice party," I said.

"I'm glad you're here," he said, taking the Seder plate from the refrigerator, the boiled egg rolling off onto the tile floor.

"Need help?" I asked, picking the shank bone off the counter.

"Remember that Seder when you tried to bake shehakol?" he said. In a minute I was back in another kitchen, separating 13 egg whites, completely baffled at how to make a dessert without flour.

"I remember," I said, the moment between us tacked to the corkboard, held still for us to observe. We were joined in a singular memory, from a time when we would have done anything for each other.

Johnny came into the kitchen, the moment broken. "Come see my room, Mom," Johnny said, taking my hand. I looked at Larry as if to ask if it was okay for me to go upstairs. He nodded, and Johnny scooted me away taking the steps up to his room two at a time. "Here's my bed," he said, a eight-year-old docent. The room was blue, a framed Derek Jeter jersey hung above the headboard. Autographed baseballs were lined up in individual display cases on the dresser. Johnny hopped on his bed, and I sat next to him.

"Can we have a sleepover tonight, Mom?" he said.

"Not tonight, Champ," I said.

After the tour, Johnny and I went back downstairs for dinner. My children, stepchildren, ex-husband and husband sat down to matzo ball soup in steamy porcelain bowls; matzo ball soup had always been a favorite of mine, the item I craved through each of my pregnancies. I had not had it in years. The smell of broth and parsley sifted through me, the lilies pushed their necks up out from the lips of the vase.

Johnny, the youngest at the table, started the Seder with the first of the four questions.

Ma nishtana ha-laila ha-zeh mi-kol ha-lelot?

"Why is this night different from all other nights?"

Mazel Tov

I stood in the driveway sipping chardonnay from a lime green plastic cup, my ex husband Larry's family entering my yard by the carload for Sophia's bat mitzvah. I greeted my former in-laws, who I had not seen in many years, with a forced smile, sweat drops the size of pearls on my forehead, the June day hot. "This is my husband Eric," I said, my voice dry as I made the awkward introductions.

"Mazel tov," they said shaking our hands.

Getting to Sophia's bat mitzvah day was hard for me. Though not court mandated, since Sophia lives with me, I often drove her to meetings with the tutor and cantor. On one of those rides she rehearsed her Torah portion. I was stunned, my daughter speaking in tongues, completely inaccessible to me. I couldn't tell if she made mistakes in her reading or not. "Very good, honey," I said, feeling the distance between us though she sat right beside me.

Many months earlier, also in the car, Sophia and I had discussed banquet halls for the bat mitzvah party. "Can we have it at our house?" Sophia had asked. I pulled off the road. "You want to have it at our house?" I said. She stared at me and in that moment I would have done anything for her. She had suffered most from the religious indecision Larry and I kept on a steady boil, no doubt feeling she was choosing sides, though she had not made the choice. "Of course we can have it at the house," I said rising to the occasion myself, though I knew I'd be planning an event that would highlight my loss, that would be a public display of her being raised Jewish not Catholic.

I took her hand, and decided then that while the ceremony was for Sophia and Larry, the party would be for Sophia and me. It would be the way I'd show my support, the way I would share in an occasion that had come to mean a lot to her.

Sophia and I worked on the invitations, the polka-dot theme. Our entire backyard was decked out in fuchsia and lime green, 300 helium balloons in the huge white tent big enough to seat 50 adults and 80 seventh-graders for dinner.

Larry stood at the other end of the tent talking to his cousins who'd flown in from Chicago. All day he and I had been careful to keep a certain physical distance between us, coming together to show solidarity only once as we posed for a photo with our daughter as she cut the cake.

I hadn't invited my Irish Catholic family to the bat mitzvah. They would have come but I did not want the added tension their attendance would bring. Catholicism meant a lot to my family. I did not want to stand next to my tear-filled mother making small talk. I invited only three close friends. "So," my friend Jess said, finding me hidden behind a maple tree in our sprawling back yard.

"Say no more," I said, "I'm not handling this well."

"Are you kidding?" Jess said, "Who else hosts a party for their ex-husband's family?"

Jess knew about the court proceedings, about my meetings with the rabbi. I thought back to those initial meetings in Rabbi

Cohen's office, Eric and I sitting on the couch holding hands, Larry and the rabbi sitting across from us. From the start of the session, I overtly tried to get Larry kicked out of the temple. "Sophia is baptized," I blurted. "I'm Catholic. We say prayers at dinner."

The rabbi was not bothered by what I am sure she perceived as nervousness. "We're open to members of different faiths," she said, her dark eyes wise, her smile genuine. "We have a lot of interfaith couples."

"But Larry and I are not an interfaith couple, we're an interfaith divorce," I said.

The rabbi commended Larry and I for agreeing on one religion for Sophia. "Parents have the duty to choose a child's religion at this age," she said. But what had been decided was not realistic. Sophia lives with me and there was no real way for me to support what the rabbi termed Sophia's Jewish identity.

As the bat mitzvah day got closer, there was the question of who would pass the Torah down to Sophia, a symbolic gesture where the Torah is passed from one generation to the next. "It's not my faith to pass on," I said, agreeing Larry alone would pass the Torah. It was the right decision but still I cried, I could not remember Sophia ever doing something significant without me being intimately involved. I hoped I'd be able to one day see the situation through a different lens that might give me perspective.

Perhaps the day had come. I caught only glimpses of Sophia at the party, she wore the satin dress we'd purchased on a trip to New York City months before, though she'd paired it with rubber boots and now walked on the stones in the river that cuts through our back yard.

Dozens of kids had joined her, the girls barefoot in their party dresses, the boys with their pants rolled up. This party would unfurl however it was supposed to. I had enough faith in God to believe that.

I looked at my daughter, surrounded by her friends, the clouds now pushed from the sky. She was having fun, and that was all that mattered. Although for different reasons, I knew this would become a day she and I would never forget.

At 13, she was already her own person, Jewish identity or not. I knew in the long term it would not be Larry or I who would decide her faith. A thoughtful strong-minded girl, Sophia would weigh the similarities and differences and choose to live her life in the way that best fit her. I hoped she would keep her balance along the way, as she did now, the sun backlighting her against the river rocks, the gold embroidered band of her dress glistening.

The Teenage Brain

The lights in the room are dim. An illustrated cross section of the brain floats on screen. "Parents of teenagers often act as surrogate frontal lobes," the speaker, a bald man with wire-rimmed spectacles says, pointing to the lateral portion behind the forehead and eye.

He explains that while the amygdala, or primitive brain, is entirely grown, the frontal lobe which governs higher processing skills such as rational thought, impulse control and goal-setting is still growing and won't fully gestate until around the age of 25.

I'd never considered being a frontal lobe part of my job description. Nor, apparently had the other parents in the packed room at our local library, eager students all, on a quest to learn more about the topic of today's seminar, the teenage brain,

I counted my five children on my fingers. In addition to Sophia and Luke, Olivia, Jamie and Johnny who would one after the other hit puberty: I'd be acting as an outsourced frontal lobe on the fly, times 5, for the next decade.

I came to the lecture because of my growing anxiety over Sophia. It had become clear to me in recent weeks that parenting a teenager requires a different skill set than parenting a small child. The lecture at the least, I hoped, would help me understand why Sophia had become, in a word, difficult, or in a phrase, a completely different child than the little tutu-wearing girl I used to tuck into pink sheets.

Not long ago, I knew every single one of Sophia's friends; she had the same six over for tea parties and trick or treat. Now, according to her Facebook page, she has 372 friends, only two of whom I recognize in the hundreds of photos Sophia displays on this website. I could spend hours tracking her online activity but I don't. I have a husband, five children, a career, a desire to sleep more than three hours a night. Plus I trust her. Does this make me a bad mother or a crazy one?

The speaker is on slide nine, which shows brain scan results. He explains that if you watch the brains of teenagers while asking them a question such as would you try to ski down Mount Rushmore, the switches in their minds would not flick and flash as much as those of an adult being asked the same question. This is because a teenager is thinking, "Yeah, I might give it a try," not weighing potential risks, while adults take all the data in and conclude: "It's not a good idea."

I broke this down in my notebook. Did this mean the same teenage boy on skis will soon be behind the wheel of a car?

The morning after my trip to the library, Sophia came downstairs for school wearing a tank top, short shorts and Ugg boots. In March. "You can't wear that to school," I said. "Why mom? Why?" she cried. "Because you can't," I said and she blasted past me, right back upstairs.

Left breathless at the breakfast table, I thought "What the heck?" I followed her into the girls' bathroom, a room I avoid at all costs. Nothing has a cap in there, toothpaste smears the sink, dirty clothes on the floor come so close to the hamper—mere millimeters really. Sophia pulled the skin under her eye to apply eyeliner. "Change your clothes first," I said flatly.

Then I summoned my frontal lobe. "If you wear shorts to school in March you will be cold, and if you wear a top like that every boy at school will be looking down your shirt," I said. The voice of reason. She looked at me as if she was going to spit then slammed the bathroom door, just like in a movie.

She came back downstairs in jeans, texting on her cell phone while breaking off small pieces of pop tart. "Who are you texting?" I asked. "Are they eating breakfast, too?" I wonder if my daughter was typing out an SOS: PLEASE SAVE ME FROM MY MOTHER.

Sophia nearly missed the bus. "Where's your sweatshirt?" I said as she raced out the screen door. I hate her going to school angry, hate going to my office wondering what I did wrong. I can lose a morning rethinking what I should have said, wondering if I was too hard on her, too easy. No seminar can help me with this.

She is, after all, the daughter who not long ago drank from a sippy cup in feety pajamas with a princess pattern, left notes for the fairies in the fireplace, and pranced about in pantyhose putting on fashion shows. Even now, there are times when she'll let me brush her long hair, smooth as sealskin. I yelled out the door after her again, "I love you, Peanut," the nickname I've had for her since I saw her take the shape of a peanut on the ultrasound.

That afternoon she came home, tossed her backpack onto the couch, sat on top of it and started in. "Can I go to the movies tonight?" she asked. Not only did the movie start at 9:00, but it was a school night. I remind myself she can't think logically yet, her impulse is to want to go, so she simply asks me, not thinking it through.

"No, you can't," I said.

"Cindy and Lindsey are going," Sophia began.

Once again, I become a frontal lobe. "If you go to a late movie on a school night, you will be overtired for school in the morning." I get the eyeroll. I head out the front door to greet the next bus.

"But can I go tonight?" she asks. I take a breath. I would have to go back to my notes. Did the frontal lobe control hearing as well?

That night I call my mother. "You were the same way as a teenager," she says, her voice tired, as if she may still be weary from having raised me. "It's going to get worse before it gets better." It's after 10:00 pm when I hang up. Sophia is sitting with her laptop on the living room floor, working on the ancient civilizations project that was assigned six weeks ago, but is due tomorrow. She has seven pages of notes, no report. I could lecture her on the necessity of planning ahead, but I don't. I'm too tired to be the voice of reason, instead I sit down on the floor, next to this little big girl I love, pencil behind her ear, her long hair sailing down her back — and I hug her, each of us a work in progress.

My Husband, The Chef

My husband eyes me as I plug in the crockpot. He does not say, "Not again, honey," even though he knows what's coming, the same meal I make every Monday. The one night I cook. Slow cooker stew—beef, carrots, onions and cream of mushroom soup—served with rice or noodles, the only part I vary. I'm a dedicated crockpot user.

"It cooks all day while the cooks away," I say to Eric with a wink. Then we're both off to work.

I don't have the attention span to cook well, to watch pots on various burners. "What's burning?" Eric will reflexively ask, even when I'm simply scrambling eggs. I'm ashamed at how stricken I am in the kitchen. I've had public catastrophes, most notably my first Thanksgiving with Eric's family, marshmallows flaming atop blackened sweet potatoes.

I've tried over the years to improve. Once, I attended an Italian cooking class where we made pasta from scratch, something I imagined a great grandmother on my father's side must have done. Inspired after the eight-week class, I went to Williams Sonoma and purchased a top-notch pasta machine. A contraption that, having never been used, came in handy one snow day as a toy to flatten play dough.

My ineptness in the kitchen only highlights Eric's culinary prowess. I take after my mother, queen of the one-dish meal, and her mother, my grandmother, who was known, on more than one occasion, to ruin a baked potato. Eric, however, is held to higher standards: he hails from a family of fine cooks; they refer to string beans as haricot vert. He plans our meals and reads cookbooks straight through, the way I read novels. On the rare occasion we don't have every ingredient in our kitchen, Eric makes something savory simply from Panko breadcrumbs and some stray zucchini.

He is a master of haute cuisine, a man who, unbelievably to me, sees cooking as a way to relax at the end of the day. He's empowered when ensconced in our small but professionally clad kitchen, no doubt happy knowing he will nourish our large family, giving us all a daily dose of love. I am in awe—and possibly jealous—of his talent.

But Eric and I clash in the kitchen. Eric is the most easygoing man I know except when surrounded by heirloom tomatoes and fresh basil. We agree on the importance of family dinners—which we sit down to every night with our five children—but our approach is different. For me the gatherings are more about spending time together. Chicken nuggets, though not pretty on the plate, are fine. For Eric, family dinner is more about sitting down to a real repast.

It's Tuesday, a school night. Eric, classically handsome with his thick hair the same color as our stainless steel appliances, makes a red wine reduction sauce. "I'd rather drink it than reduce it," I say. I don't see the sense in taking two hours and twelve pans to make a meal that will be eaten in a flat six minutes, so I nudge him. "What time are we eating?" I ask. I am antsy and hungry, it's after 7:00, and I'm ready to get the kids to bed.

My husband takes his time, surely wanting to eat earlier, but he can't help himself in the process. He clarifies the butter, stuffs and sautés, debones and deglazes. He inhabits his ingredients, considers texture along with taste, the panache of colors on the plate. I watch as he peels the skin off a tomato, and I wonder if the amount of care that goes into a meal really does matter, if fine dining every night will impact my children in years to come.

I try to move things along. I make the mistake of offering to help. "I'll dice" I say, the inept sous chef. And though I have diced many times before, Eric shows me again, setting me up with a cutting board and Henckel's pro paring knife.

Then I remember. "I bought these," I say, taking out the pre-diced onions I got at Stop 'n Shop.

"I don't think so, honey," he says, gently pushing me aside.

It is 8:15. I ring the dinner bell, our five kids straggle in, somewhat unaware of the culinary artistry of which they are about to partake: spinach-stuffed rib-eye roast, potato-mushroom gratin and fennel confit. The children take their place at the table. "This looks amazing," Luke says. "I'm starving," Johnny says. Eric serves the meal. Each dish is a plate-sized still life. Perhaps the careful preparation does make a difference, even though it's almost bedtime. I give a toast to Eric now as I do each night.

"Thank you for cooking," I say. And I mean it. Every time.

Empanada Day

"I'll make the dough this year," I tell Nelly on the phone. I'm determined, though my talents flourish nowhere near the kitchen.

"I like Nelly's empanadas," Olivia says when I hang up.

"Don't make them, Mom," Sophia adds.

In the morning we will drive two hours to Nelly's house for Empanada Day, a self-declared holiday we've been celebrating the Sunday before Thanksgiving for twelve years now.

"Nelly always does everything, it's time I took a turn," I say, unsure about tampering with our tradition. But Nelly had a hard year, suffering with health issues, and I want to do this for her.

I start the dough making immediately. "Get the scrapbooks," I tell Olivia. Flipping through pages of Empanada Days over the years, I look at the pictures of the girls smushing balls of dough in their high chairs. The note, scribbled beneath the step-by-step photos, says: about half a cup of shortening for every three or four cups of flour. I have no idea how much water and vinegar to actually add, so I continue to guesstimate the recipe that lives in Nelly's heart, not within the pages of a scrapbook. "We can do this, girls."

Nelly and I met more than a decade ago. She was the first and last person to come into my kitchen when I interviewed for caregivers. Back to work, I was in need of childcare for Olivia and Sophia, who were then just 6 weeks and 18 months old. Nelly lived with us during the week. A few years after she came I had my son, Johnny – Juanito, as Nelly called him.

Johnny hung on my hip the morning I told Nelly I was getting divorced, I'd been up all night and the tears dropped into my cold black coffee. Nelly, herself a single mother of three grown children helped us through the excruciating loss and a yearlong custody battle. When it was all over, the kids and I moved from New Jersey to Connecticut, but Nelly stayed in New Jersey. Six years have passed since Nelly lived with us, and in that time Sophia and Olivia have been bridesmaids in Nelly's daughter's wedding, and I'm aunt to Nelly's grandchildren. Even though we no longer share our day-to-days, Nelly is still our Nelly, and Empanada Day still stands.

Empanadas, a South American delicacy, are little meat-filled pouches the shape of half-moons. The name Empanada comes from the Spanish verb *empanar*, meaning to wrap or coat in bread. Many cultures have versions of the empanada—The English call them pasties. The Italians call them calzones. In the Caribbean they're known as pastelitos. But in Bolivia, where Nelly was born, they're empanadas. Since I have no recipes passed down from my Irish-Italian family, I've borrowed from Nelly and her Bolivian roots.

I scoop cups of flour into a mound on the counter—no mixing bowl. I make a well in the center, volcano style, just like the photo. "Is this right?" I ask Sophia, as Olivia cracks three eggs into the well. Sophia adds the Crisco shortening, and a big pinch of salt, and I add some water and vinegar and then attempt to knead the mixture into a ball of dough the size of a football. But the consistency is way off. It's mucky, sticky. I add more flour and the powder falls on the floor in fistfuls. I panic, add more flour, the ball growing.

"You should have let Nelly do it," the girls say, laughing now.

On the drive to Nelly's house the next morning, I pull over and the girls and I run into the Stop 'N Shop looking for the Goya aisle. Feeling useless that I have to resort to store-bought, I put the premade empanada dough in the cart. I'm stoic at the checkout line; the girls know not to say anything.

"Mine didn't work," I blurt when we enter Nelly's house and pass her the plastic grocery bag with the dough. It's as if Nelly has expected this: she takes us into the kitchen of her tiny apartment with kisses. "Come my muñeca," she says to Sophia and Olivia, and maybe me too, her little dolls. "No importa. I do it," she says pulling the canister of flour from the cabinet. She is small, the same height as Sophia, her black hair cut into a bob at her chin, her dark skin smooth as a wine bottle.

Nelly is efficient, quick with her movements from sink to counter. She once again works too fast for me to transfer her spontaneous measurements to my head. The flour mound is formed, the eggs folded in, the ball of dough ready to be rolled out. Nelly gives Olivia and Sophia each a rolling pin.

Nelly made the filling last night, a detailed mixture that includes meat with olives, hard boiled egg, and potatoes, all diced to the size of green peas. The girls and Nelly put a spoonful of meat in the center of each flat four-inch circle and set to work folding the circles into crescents, crimping the rounded side by hand, so the meat won't ooze when Nelly fries the thin pouches. I have to crimp with a fork, I can't pinch the edges the way they do.

As Nelly's hands seal the dough, I think of her in the kitchen of my old house, making arroz con pollo, the girls playing with letter magnets, sticking them on the fridge. I remember those long days coming home from work late, running upstairs to see the children, bathed and smelling of baby powder, curled up on Nelly's bed, watching Spanish soap operas. I remember the nights when Sophia was learning to read, and Nelly practiced her English along side her. All those Frog and Toad books.

The kitchen smells of cumin and olives. Nelly fries the dough in a pot of hot oil. She removes each pouch with a slotted spoon and places the crispy crowns on a paper towel.

I sip coffee, watching Nelly and Sophia and Olivia work. Maybe it's just as well I wasn't able to make the dough. The pleasure of seeing Nelly with my daughters, her hands over their hands as they roll, makes me as happy as I have ever been. And I know it will be my girls, not me, who will make the dough in the future, when Nelly and I are old, and we all gather for Empanada Day.

Facebook

"Clean up your Facebook page or I'll post a message on your wall," I text my daughter on Saturday morning. Sophia is at her father's house for the weekend. I imagine her in bed, her long black hair in a tangle, sleeping on her stomach, bum in the air, just as she did when she as a baby.

I go online a few hours later to see if she has taken down the objectionable language. She has. So I don't—this time—post a message such as "Stop talking trash," on her wall for all her friends to see.

On Sunday when she comes home, she throws her knapsack on the couch and immediately goes to the computer. I shoo her off—it's time for a talk.

"You know, everything you do online affects your reputation," I say, showing her an article about college admissions offices checking applicant's Facebook pages. "Do you want to get into a good college? Mrs. Dover can see what you post," I go on. "If she sees bad language on your wall, do you think she'll ask you to babysit anymore?" This more immediate example warrants a pause; Sophia stops fiddling with her phone long enough for me to finish.

My daughter joined Facebook a year ago, when she was 12. I didn't think too much of it. I only told her to "friend" me, so I could see what she posted on her profile. It was true that all her friends were on, and at first it seemed to me a good way to share homework assignments.

Permitting Sophia to graduate from Club Penguin, a kids gaming site, to Facebook was a huge parenting mistake. She quickly became a slave to the site, checking her profile page a dozen times a day, "friending" people promiscuously, racking up 456 friends almost overnight. "Facebook dilutes friendship," I said. "What you post is seen by your friends and their friends and their friends' friends."

I rarely use Facebook; I go on really just to see what Sophia is up to, and I can't check too often; I have four other children I also need to parent. I'm not a fan of social networking, because I'd rather see people I truly care about in person, and I can't find the time to respond to online invitations to connect with high school sweethearts or my long lost trigonometry teacher.

But I can see the appeal for teenagers. On one hand, Facebook helps them forget their social awkwardness, to hide behind their online selves, able to say anything they want to say. On the other hand, the site is a huge online popularity contest, with winners and losers and a lot of mean kids.

The more I'm on Facebook, the more worried I become; yesterday there was a flashing ad for fake ID services. And I read a news article citing that Facebook may cause depression. Apparently being electronically de-friended can take a toll on teenagers for obvious reasons. In my day, it was hard enough to endure lunchroom gossip, and now such gossip is posted for the masses to see. I can't imagine anything worse as a teenager.

We are at the kitchen table, and Sophia looks busy,

seemingly doing homework, blogging for social studies on her laptop. "Dylan likes me," she says, elated, showing me the comment on her Facebook page.

"It's homework time," I say.

Deep down, I wish I'd polyurethaned her at age six, when she was not yet tainted by technology, when she went to her best friend's birthday party at Ruby's Candy Shop and I took pictures of her among the pink- and lavender-colored candies—my small sweet girl, who did not persecute me for taking a picture.

Now she takes her own pictures from her cell phone and posts them on her Facebook page. My beautiful daughter, modeling a bathing suit from the fitting room at Abercrombie, a suit way too sexy for her age. I see now what she does when I allow her to stay in one store with her friend while I shop in another store. I rage at her. "It's common sense what should and should not go on your page!" I howl. She takes down the photos.

Not long after that episode, Sophia posted bad language on her page again. But I didn't know it at first; she'd put a filter on my email address so I was blocked from seeing certain posts. Somehow she forgot to filter out my husband. He saw the language and after dinner that night we spoke to Sophia. Instead of the calm discussion I had planned, I found myself shouting. "You can't filter your mother. I'm un-filterable!" We took her computer away, and it was as if we had cut off five of her fingers.

For the rest of the week she sulked in ways only a teenage girl can sulk. She brooded about the house, no eye contact, ear buds in her ears, completely tuned out. After the sulking phase, she went into begging, saying that she needed the laptop for homework.

She's earned her computer back. But I'm thinking of posting a comment on her wall: I love you, I'll type, so all her friends can see.

Divvying Up The Days

This morning, an email from my ex-husband: If you get the 24th through the 2nd that's 10 days, which leaves the split at 10 to 6.

This is how Larry and I discuss divvying up vacation time with our three kids. Matter-of-fact emails. Our children checkers we move from square to square on some imaginary game board, keeping close track of how long they stay on each side.

I have Christmas and New Year's this year, I email back, my fingers jabbing at the keyboard, livid that Larry wants additional days with the children. We have been splitting our parenting time according to a Property Settlement Agreement signed years ago when we divorced, and the scheduling is still grueling.

You had Thanksgiving I email, feeling he's deliberately trying to make it impossible for me to make plans for the winter break. I have to buy the plane tickets I write. He does not respond, the emails suddenly stop, giving me time to marinate in my anger. I will not call him. A direct conversation would be worse, my emotions would be amplified by anger and I'd tell him I'm going to call my lawyer—always my default line. Or his.

At work, I try to calm down, holding the warm coffee mug in my hands, but my nerves seem exposed. My hands shake a little. I organize the junk in my desk drawers, sorting and tossing and thinking of Larry, the man I once married and had children with, who I now wish would just go away, though I know we are knotted in each other's lives forever, as parents of the same three kids.

That night I lie in bed with my husband, who has an ex-wife we deal with, and Luke and Jamie who are also on co-parenting schedules. "I envy couples who got it right the first time," I say, considering the swarms of normal parents who don't have to separate from their young children on holidays.

I stare at the ceiling, a thin streak of moonlight smearing my nightstand. "Should I buy the plane tickets?" I ask Eric, and fall into sleep, my eyes half open all night as if my face has been starched. I dream my ex-husband does not bring the children back to me in time and we miss the flight.

The next day, I wake at 5:00 to check email, to see what Larry has to say, but there are no new emails. Worse, in a few hours I will have to see him for Johnny's fourth-grade teacher conference.

At Cider Mill School, Mrs. Tate, her blonde hair loose around her face, Johnny's first crush, meets us at the classroom door. Larry and I sit on the kid-sized plastic chairs around a circle table and I try to keep my face, my attitude, neutral. Mrs. Tate shows us Johnny's short story The Frog Who Wanted to Fly. Rather than consider its content, I'm thinking how I need to be the one to take the story home for Johnny's baby book. I want to sneak it into my bag now.

"Johnny also did a wonderful job on his social studies and science projects," Mrs. Tate says. I look at my ex-husband with a look that says I'm the one who did those assignments with Johnny, don't you dare take any credit. I consider the field trip to the aquarium that I chaperoned, the science experiment two nights ago, a Mentos mint dropped in a Coke bottle that produced a ten-foot geyser in our kitchen.

While Mrs. Tate talks, I keep a silent tally of what homework gets done at my house and what homework gets done at Larry's. In doing so, I miss some of what she says and I wither in my little seat as I become aware on some level of my petty thinking.

"I just love having Johnny in my class. He's a super kid," Mrs. Tate says making direct eye contact first with me then with Larry. I don't even want Mrs. Tate to look at Larry, to consider him, to think he had a part in anything that might have made Johnny smart and good-natured.

We sit for a bit longer, looking at Johnny's standardized test scores, his self-portrait, and then his family tree, complete with both my family and Larry's. I think of Larry's mother, who I love, and his father, a mathematician, who I never met. I consider Johnny's love of math, so much like his grandfather and father. My small thoughts crack enough to let some other possibilities filter in. I consider this man who was supposed to be my forever. I look at his eyes and see my son in them.

And I know that I'm not solely responsible for the boy Johnny has become. My ex has something to do with it. I can't pinpoint what exactly, but I'm willing to admit for a moment that he's Johnny's father and he makes a contribution. I focus in then on what Mrs. Tate is saying instead of the sharp words from the emails Larry and I have been sending. My emotions flip. For the moment, I'm no longer obsessed with who has what day with the children. I'm thinking about Johnny being a well-adjusted little boy, and how perhaps Larry and I, though our behavior is often bad, have not done so badly.

"He's a great kid. We did something right," I say to Larry as we leave the school and walk to our separate cars in the parking lot, the morning gray and windy, the leaves blowing off the trees, unsettled.

The Dance

The teenage girls unpack from cars wearing thigh-high glitter dresses with the backs cut out. It's Sophia's first high school dance. We wait in the parking lot for her best friend, Lisa. "Text Lisa and make sure she's coming," I say, not wanting Sophia to go in alone. I know what it's like, the first big high school dance. I feel as though I can touch the narrow frame of Sophia's life, that we are somehow tied together on this cold October night.

More girls than boys enter the school, and they look so big compared to Sophia, who has always been the smallest in her class. I am nervous for her—her having fun, her fitting in — but she does not seem concerned. She's wearing denim shorts and a sparkle shirt, her own version of dress-up. I had asked her to try on dresses before we came, and she did, looking beautiful, her small frame etched with sequins. I didn't push too much. I had my chance to dress her up when she was a girl, the apple-patterned dress on her first day of kindergarten, the patent leather shoes every Easter. She is not mine to fashion anymore. Her life orbits somewhere west of mine.

In the dark from the passenger seat Sophia grabs my arm. "That's Dylan," she whispers. "Oh my God, Dylan!" she says a little louder. I've been hearing about Dylan since school started six weeks ago.

"He's handsome," I say, noting the tall boy with dark hair, khaki pants and a blue button-down shirt.

"Cute, Mom," Sophia corrects, and pulls down the car visor. She is either checking her maroon lipstick in the mirror, or hiding her face from Dylan, or not wanting to be seen with me.

"You're beautiful," I say, and she acts like she does not hear me.

Watching Dylan walk into the school, I think of the boy I fell in love with at my first high school dance when I, too, was 14. A kindling of memory, images rewind in my mind: the crepe-papered gymnasium of my Catholic high school, my pink calf-length dress, Jimmy Middleton walking across the dance floor to tell me that Danny Demarco liked me. "If Danny asked you to dance would you say yes?" Jimmy had asked.

"Yes" I whispered. That yes changed my life that night. Danny, an upperclassman, liked me. He would become the boy I would date for many years and love for many more, until eventually we lost track of each other.

I kissed Danny at that dance, in the storage room behind the gym. "Can I?" he had asked.

"Just once," I said, nervous that Sister Maryanne would find us. I went home that night and checked my lips in the mirror to see if I could tell where he kissed.

I look at Sophia in the seat next to me and wondered if her life would change tonight, if a certain boy would carve a spot on her heart like Danny did mine. "What do you like about Dylan?" I ask.

"Oh Mom," she says, "please." Maybe Dylan and Sophia will dance, I think, but then wonder if boys ask girls to dance any more, or if they just text each other from across the room.

I consider telling Sophia about Danny, the boy I thought I would marry, then wonder if girls even think inside fairytales anymore. Marriage. Happily ever after. Sophia wants to design jewelry and live in New York City. I could see her staying single for a long time, possibly forever. I pull my mind back in; she's only 14.

Sophia's friend Lisa knocks on the window of our car and Sophia darts out. "Hi, Mrs. Soviero," Lisa says.

"You girls have fun. Be safe," I say. I am the cut-out mother now, with an ounce of the girl I was still inside of me, Danny picking me up on in his old Ford Taurus Thursdays after school, the two of us in his room, cross-legged on the blue shag carpet, listening to Billy Joel records, the song "Only the Good Die Young" playing over and over again.

I pull out of the parking lot, trees swaying in the corners of the night. I'm already anxious to return for the pick-up. I imagine Sophia getting in the car, rubbed with her own memories—memories that, years from now, when she's in her 40s, might come back to her on a cold October night, full force.

Sisters. Daughters.

"You did the right thing," I say, handing the mugs of warm milk and honey to Sophia and Olivia, who sit cross-legged on the floor of their bedroom, laptops open to Facebook.

A freshman in high school, Sophia broke up with her boyfriend Adam, whom she dated for six months, a few hours ago at the library. I picked her up and couldn't wait to get her home to Olivia, who I knew would find the right things to say.

"Maybe I shouldn't have done it," Sophia says, back at home, sipping the warm milk, crying again. Her fine-drawn face is too pale, her long dark hair falling in shower-damp wisps over her eyes.

"But you've been wanting to break up for a month," Olivia says. "You'll be happy about this tomorrow." Olivia puts her arm around Sophia's shoulder, and plucks an Oreo cookie from the plate. She's got this under control, I can tell. And I am grateful, not for the first time, that my girls have each other.

I wonder if I even need to be here but I am enjoying my

dark-haired daughters with matching dimples. I love watching them comfort each other, these daughters that I always wanted. These sisters, each who they are in part because of the other.

I remember a life before them, but they don't remember a life without each other. When Sophia met Olivia in the hospital hours after Olivia was born, Sophia poked her infant sister on the nose. "Mine!" Sophia said. "Mine, Mommy," she said again. Then she shouted, "Boo!"—Olivia's nickname even now.

It was Sophia's hand Olivia grabbed for when she took her first steps in the kitchen of our old house. "Mommy, she bobbled!" Sophia had screamed, at the ripe age of three, as Olivia toddled two steps.

When they were very young we spent evenings home alone, my husband out or away much of the time. We'd play sink-or-float in the master bathtub, me balanced on the side of the tub throwing small items into the bubbly water, a coin or plastic Easter egg, and the girls shrieking "Sink!" or "Float!" depending on the object. After the tub, Sophia would dress Olivia in my pantyhose, princess pajamas and a plastic tiara. "It's a fashion show," Sophia would tell Olivia, pointing her toward the long hall that served as the runway.

When their father and I got divorced. We told them over breakfast on a hot July morning. "Mommy and Daddy aren't going to be married any more. We don't belong together," I had said.

"Are you sad?" Sophia asked, then, "Can we go out and play now?" She took Olivia's hand and they raced to the jungle gym in our backyard, the sun bright, their shoulders small. Sophia pushed Olivia on the swing. "Kick the clouds!" Sophia shouted.

The hardest part was letting go of my girls when they spent weekends with their father. Sophia would pack the backpacks, zip Olivia's coat and snap her into the car seat of her father's red Jeep. Once Sophia ran back inside. "Mommy" she said, "Olivia needs her head medicine." I pulled the bottle of Children's Motrin from the cabinet and gave it to Sophia, amazed how she'd remembered and I had not. Away at their father's house, they had to make do without me, and they did well. I pictured them racing through the rooms of their father's large house, playing with Molly and Holly, their baby dolls. They were sisters in the same situation. I told myself they'd be just fine. I had given them to each other.

The girls have their own rooms at our house and at their father's but still they share a room. "We share clothes anyway," Olivia says, when I ask why she doesn't use her own room. Size-wise they can share clothes but rarely do anymore; Sophia now leans toward all shades of black jeans and retro band T-shirts while Olivia likes to wear colors and shirts with collars.

On school nights my daughters do the dinner dishes together—one washes, one dries. They sing along to their Ramones playlist. "Your turn to scrub pots," Olivia says, and Sophia bangs two saucepans together, and they laugh. I watch from the family room, enjoying the girls they have become not exactly what I had imagined, but better.

Now in her soft-lit bedroom, Sophia picks up her guitar, starts to play some notes from the song her boyfriend Adam wrote for her.

"Don't do that," Olivia says, "you'll make the hurt worse." I brush the cookie crumbs onto the saucer, clear the milk mugs and give them each a hug before leaving. Sometimes I want to do it all over again, go back to each of their births, but the years have played out well, I think, and my girls are right where they should be—with each other.

The Script

The music rumbled, my body pulsed to the beat of the bass. My kids, Luke and Sophia, 15 and 14, were somewhere in the crowd, much closer to the band than me.

I stood by the bar sipping vodka from a plastic cup with hundreds of other people. I hung in the back of the Roseland Ballroom, a New York City concert landmark with no assigned seats just a huge concrete floor. I'd not been to a concert in the city in 20 years since my days of bar-hopping in grad school, discovering rogue bands at The Knitting Factory. I remembered how, back then, music made me feel like a part of something.

It was hard to feel a part of this though, being a 43-year-old mother of five among people half my age. Self conscious, I took my cell phone out, but unlike every other person, I did not wave it above my head snapping photos of the band, instead I texted my husband at home. "I'm the only one wearing a turtleneck," I wrote.

When Sophia and Luke asked me months ago if we could see

The Script, I immediately said yes. I wondered why I was so quick to get the tickets to a concert in New York City on a school night. I think it was because Luke and Sophia were teenagers now, and doing something together would fill the empty space where our conversation didn't happen as often, or perhaps I just needed an excuse to spend time with them.

The band began, and suddenly I was at every concert I'd ever been to.

"Has anyone here ever dated a douchebag?" the lead singer spoke into the microphone.

"Yeah!" the crowd cooed.

"Then this song is for you," the singer said, easing into a melody filled with angst. I was shocked at first, then thought about it, considering some of the men I dated in my life and figuring what the hell, the song was for me, too, then.

"What time does The Script go on?" a girl wearing a knit hat, not much older than my daughter asked me.

I squeezed the lemon on the rim of my drink.

"I thought this was The Script," I said, embarrassed, grateful Luke and Sophia couldn't hear me. They were far away from me now, somewhere upstream where kids screamed. I had left them in front, though they had not asked me to. It was my idea to give them some space.

It was after 9:00 when The Script appeared through the smoke on stage. This time, I recognized the band leader, Danny O'Donoghue. Sophia had pointed Danny out on band videos on YouTube for weeks. I fell into the first song, which I actually knew. I relaxed, even swayed a little. A man, the only man with gray hair in the place, came up to me.

"You like The Script?" he shouted over the noise.

"I think so," I screamed back. He lingered, and I wondered if he too was a chaperone. He lingered some more, his shoulder rubbing against my chest a bit too often, and I considered that perhaps that had been a pickup line. I went into the lobby to buy Luke and Sophia band shirts.

"Is this band really that good?" the T-shirt vendor, a young guy with a tattooed arm, asked. "I mean there are a lot of hot girls here." Knowing I was not one of them, I laughed.

"They're three guys from Dublin, the lead singer's got a great smile," I said, taking the two shirts I bought and stuffing them into my oversized pocketbook. I hesitated then.

"Wait, one more," I said, and bought myself a shirt.

Despite the signs on every door that said "ALL EXITS ARE FINAL," I asked another tattooed man who was wearing a neon shirt that said STAFF if I could go outside. He stamped my hand and ushered me to the smoking exit. I was free to file out to a fenced smoking area in front of the building where I stood with 20 teenagers in the cold October night, rain drizzling down. Momentarily in touch with a younger version of myself, I bummed a cigarette from a young girl in a halter top, black shorts and purple lace tights. "Thanks," I said, and she gave me a high five.

Next door, the Broadway show Jersey Boys was letting out and the people my age hailed taxis. I should hop the fence, I thought, be with them. But instead I took a drag on the cigarette. I considered the night, my kids, the crowd. I went back in to have some fun, my hair damp from the drizzle.

Blue lights scanned the stage. The crowd roared the chorus, all at once, finding each other within the repeated rhythms; These are hard times and they're making me crazy, don't give up on me baby... I began singing. Somehow inside a favorite song, there was space enough for everyone.

I realized then that it had been more than two hours since I had seen Luke and Sophia. I tried to make my way toward the stage, spearing through the crowd, but I stopped, blocked by hundreds of people.

The band played for another hour, it was almost midnight

when the concert ended. I texted Sophia and Luke to meet me at the exit. For the first time that evening I felt panic that I wouldn't find them. But eventually I spotted them and let out the breath I'd been holding in. We walked out of the Roseland toward the parking garage in the now heavy rain.

"That was awesome," Luke said.

"Thanks so much, Mom," Sophia said, adding something about seeing Coldplay next. We were a few blocks away from the Roseland now, I drew my two teenagers close to me, and we walked up 55th Street, humming, the music already vibrating in my memory.

The Renovation

Eric and I and our kids see the stars through plastic sheathing where the roof of our home should be while we eat take-out food on the folding table. "Is that the big dipper?" Johnny asks, looking upward, scooping Chinese noodles into his mouth.

"It could be," I say.

We're eight weeks into the kitchen renovation Eric and I have been planning since we bought our circa 1842 house in Wilton, Connecticut, six years ago—when we married and chose this particular roof under which to raise our five kids. I remember the day we brought the children to see the house for the first time. "A Harry Potter closet!" Olivia, then six, had shrieked, snuggling into the space inside the stairwell.

The house seemed built for Eric and me, two artistic types. There was nothing cookie cutter in the place—every beam, every sash window, unique. It was the first house we saw and the only one we bid on. The winding back staircase, five fireplaces, and view of the Saugatuck River out back held promise. Every room was perfect—except the kitchen, which was no bigger than a walk-in closet.

Our goal with this renovation is to transform the shoebox kitchen into an eat-in model with enough space for a big kitchen table that will serve as a center for our family meals, our family life. One like I had in the childhood home I grew up in, a table long gone, where I spent long hours with my Aunt Joanne and grandmother sorting things out over coffee and Nona's crumb cake.

But for now there's a hole in the floor where my stove should be.

"There's an issue," I tell Eric when he gets home from work. I'm shouting over the staccato punch of a nail gun. "It will bump the price," I say, knowing our lives having become a continuously adjusted expense report since the project began. Eric, ever patient, listens as I tell him how Cliff, our project manager, explained the problem to me.

"When we knocked down that wall," Cliff had said pointing to the debris, "we found rot in the supporting beam." So soft was the wood holding up that section of our home that Cliff, to illustrate, stabbed a screwdriver straight into the beam and it sunk into the wood up to the handle.

"It's got to be fixed then," Eric says, matter of fact. That night he revises the numbers on our spreadsheet and I dream the corners of our kitchen crumble like a scene in a movie.

I crave the manageable chaos we had mere months ago. The well-oiled world I made for the seven of us before men with tool belts started pulling the house apart. Prior to the renovation we had a different kind of mess, dirty laundry on the floor, Oreo cookie crumbs everywhere. But now we trip over paint cans and long bands of floorboards stacked against walls. I miss the well-organized space we once had for our pots and pans that now teeter on the table in the family room, our new spot for the TV remote controls.

The kids do better than I do with the mess. Messy fits their personalities, none of the five being neat like me, all of them comfortable with things strewn everywhere. Johnny enjoys climbing over the furniture that's all squeezed into one room—it's a new game: King of the Sofa.

In my office, which is detached from the house, I organize paperclips, alphabetize my books, re-name my files, seeking order. I look out my office window and watch the men work. Today there is a yellow crane in the side yard.

I go inside for a snack, our kitchen appliances are in the middle of the family room. Another wall gets whacked, spitting dust. I hate to see the insides of my house exposed, the floorboards bruised. Maybe this old home wasn't meant to be expanded, I think, imagining the memories and moments stored within the cracks of these plaster walls. I want this to always be the place my children gather together. A place for all the family dinners, play dates, and prom photos still to come. I want the kids to come back here after their life's adventures lead them away. To return and gather around the big wooden kitchen table, well worn from years of meals and good conversation.

Marcelle Soviero is an award-winning essayist and poet. Her essays have appeared in various online and print media including The New York Times, Salon.com, Literary Mama and Eating Well. She has frequently appeared on American Public Media's syndicated radio show, The Story. She teaches essay, memoir and poetry writing in Westport, Connecticut, and lives in Wilton, Connecticut with her husband and five children. Visit the author at www.marcellesoviero.com.